EVERYDAY CONSUMER ENGLISH

SECOND EDITION

EVERYDAY CONSUMER ENGLISH

Julie Weissman
College of Lake County
Grayslake, Illinois

Howard H. Kleinmann

Revised by Louisa Rogers

National Textbook Company
a division of NTC/CONTEMPORARY PUBLISHING COMPANY
Lincolnwood, Illinois USA

Acknowledgments

This book was developed in part by the Allegheny Intermediate Unit, Pittsburgh, PA, as *Project Face* (Howard H. Kleinmann, Project Director; Julie Weissman, Curriculum Specialist) with a grant from the Office of Consumers' Education, U.S. Office of Education, Department of Health, Education, and Welfare.

Book design and composition: Don Williams

Illustrations: Helen Daniels

Contents

Unit 1 **Budgets**

Unit 2 **Banking – Savings Accounts**

Unit 3 Banking – Checking Accounts

Unit 4 Supermarkets

Unit 5 Supermarket Shopping

Unit 6 Looking for an Apartment

Unit 7 Renting an Apartment

Unit 8 Buying Furniture and Appliances

Preface

Everyday Consumer English, Second Edition is designed for individuals who want to improve their English-language skills while developing selected consumer life-skills. The premise of the book is that in order to be able to function effectively in American society, students of English must be able to apply their developing language skills in meaningful contexts in situations they are likely to encounter every day.

This book is designed for students who have mastered some of the basics of English in the skill areas of listening, speaking, reading, and writing but who still need to become more fully functional in everyday activities. Specifically, the contents presuppose student knowledge of the following basic English structures: simple present tense; present continuous; *going to* + verb for the future; imperatives; *can, want,* and *need* + *to* + verb. These structures are reviewed in Unit One.

The book is divided into eight units. Each unit contains a general consumer-education theme. The language material in each unit is covered against the background of the unit's consumer theme. Therefore, as students are being introduced to English-language material, they are also being exposed to consumer information that they need in order to function competently in American society. This dual focus on developing linguistic competence and functional consumer competence is the distinguishing characteristic of this book.

Key features of the units include the following:

Learner objectives, which specify the target consumer and language competencies of each unit as well as the vocabulary items.

Dialogues, which introduce consumer topics and target structures to be covered in the unit.

Comprehension questions on the dialogues reinforcing the consumer theme of the unit and the target structures.

Grammar practice in communicative and functional contexts related to the consumer theme of the unit. Exercises are varied and proceed from controlled types to less controlled types. Simplified grammatical explanations with examples are provided.

Reading exercises focusing on basic consumer information and reinforcing target grammatical material.

Listening comprehension exercises designed to help the student develop aural skills necessary for functioning effectively as a consumer.

Problem-solving activities in selected units that require the student to tap language and consumer knowledge simultaneously in order to make prudent consumer decisions.

In an easy-to-use format, *Everyday Consumer English* contains a variety of stimulating communicative activities aimed at improving speaking, reading, writing, and listening skills, all in the context of general consumer themes. This *Second Edition* reflects changes in prices and practices, making it an up-to-date and reliable resource.

Budgets

 Learner Objectives

Consumer Competencies
- Leaning what a budget is
- Learning how to plan a family or individual budget
- Learning how to use a budget

Grammatical Structures
- Review of the following structures: simple present tense; present continuous; *going to* + verb for the future; imperatives
- Being able to understand and use the following structures: *can, want,* and *need* + *to* + verb

Vocabulary Items
- Being able to understand and use the following words in context:

Nouns		Verbs	Adjectives
accident	expense	average	angry
ad	insurance	budget	medical
advertisement	Laundromat	complain	
amount	laundry	confuse	
appliance	lease	decrease	
architect	loan	include	
average	payment	register	
bank account	repair	rent	
bill	steak	save	
budget	take-home pay	spend	
consumer	tax		
dryer	washing machine		
emergency			

 **Reading**

Jerome Wilson's in the public library. He's putting up an advertisement about a class in consumer education. He's going to teach the Consumer Education class. Mr. Wilson's going to put up the ad in many places—in supermarkets, shopping centers, Laundromats and at the university. Tomorrow, the ad is going to be in the newspaper.

Here's the ad:

Do you spend a lot of money every month?
Do you get angry about the high cost of living?
Do you know how to open a bank account, rent an apartment, buy furniture?
Do advertisements and leases confuse you?

Come to the Consumer Education class

You can learn to:

- Budget your money.
- Spend less and save more.
- Save money at the supermarket.
- Rent an apartment.
- Buy furniture and appliances.
- Understand advertisements and leases.

You can learn to be a good consumer!

TIME: ..... 8–10 P.M., Tuesdays and Thursdays

PLACE: ...... Continental Community College
Call Continental Community College to register.

PHONE: 654-7900

■ Comprehension Questions

1. What's a consumer? Who's a consumer?

   _____

2. Where's Mr. Wilson?

   _____

3. What's he doing?

   _____

4. Who's going to teach the Consumer Education class?

   _____

5. Where's Mr. Wilson going to put up the ad?

   _____

6. What can you learn in the Consumer Education class?

   _____

7. When and where's the Consumer Education class?

   _____

8. How can you register for the Consumer Education class?

   _____

 # Grammar

Tense Review: Present; Present Continuous; *Going to* + Verb for the Future; Imperatives

A. Read about Nilda.

> Nilda's at home. She's watching TV. Her father is reading the newspaper. He sees the ad for the Consumer Education class.
>
> **Nilda's father** Nilda, here's a class for you and Charlie. It's a good class to take before you get married.

> **Nilda** (*Reading the ad*) "Learn to budget your money; learn to spend less and save more." Charlie and I need this class. He always complains because he can't save money. Everything is so expensive! I'm going to call right away.

Ask your classmates about their activities. Follow the example. Answer with a short answer.

Example: Nilda's watching TV.
Are you watching TV?

<u>No, I'm not.</u>

1. Nilda's father is reading the newspaper.
   Are you reading the newspaper?

   _____

2. Nilda wants to learn to budget her money.
   Do you want to learn to budget your money?

   _____

3. Charlie always complains because he can't save money.
   Do you always complain because you can't save money?

   _____

B. Read about Quan and Mayling.

> Quan and Mayling are shopping at the supermarket. Mayling sees the ad for the Consumer Education class.
>
> **Mayling** Quan, here's the perfect class for us! "Learn to save money at the supermarket."
>
> **Quan** "Learn to budget your money." You're right, Mayling. We need to budget our money. We need to save money for the baby.
>
> **Mayling** Let's register right away.

Ask your classmates about their activities. Follow the examples. Form questions. Answer them with a short answer.

Example: Quan and Mayling are shopping at the supermarket.

<u>Are you shopping at the supermarket?</u>

<u>No, I'm not.</u>

1. Mayling wants to learn to save money at the supermarket.

_____

_____

2. Quan wants to learn to budget their money.

_____

_____

3. Quan and Mayling need to save money for their baby.

_____

_____

4. Quan and Mayling are going to register for the Consumer Education class.

_____

_____

C. Read about Althea.

> Althea's going to paint the kitchen in her apartment. She's putting newspaper on the floor. She sees the ad for the Consumer Education class.
>
> **Althea** (_Thinking_) Hmmmm. This class looks interesting. "Learn to rent an apartment. Learn to understand advertisements and leases." I need a new apartment. I'm tired of this one. I always need to paint or fix it. I'm going to register for this class.

Ask your classmates about their activities. Follow the example. Form questions. Answer them with a short answer.

Example: Althea's going to paint her kitchen.

   Are you going to paint your kitchen?

   Yes, I am.

1. Althea needs a new apartment.

_____

_____

2. Althea's tired of her apartment.

_____

_____

3. Althea always needs to paint or fix her apartment.

_____

_____

4. Althea wants to register for the Consumer Education class.

_____

_____

D. Read about budgets.

> The Consumer Education class is learning about budgets. A budget is a plan for the use of your money. It can help you spend your money. It can also help you save money.

Althea's making a budget. How much does she spend a month? Ask questions to find out. Follow the examples.

Example: Rent

How much does Althea spend a month on rent?

$500/month

She spends $500 a month on rent.

1. Food

_____

$200/month

_____

2. Rental insurance

_____

$132/year $132 ÷ 12 = $_____/month

_____

3. Gas for her car

_____

$15/week $15 x 4 = $_____/month

_____

4. Car insurance

_____

$750/year $750 ÷ 12 = $_____/month

_____

Example: Electric bill

How much is Althea's electric bill a month?

$53.36/month

Her electric bill is $53.36 a month.

1. Gas bill

_____

$13.21/month

_____

2. Water bill

_____

$24.00/two months $24.00 ÷ 2 = $_____/month

_____

3. Telephone bill

_____

$41.00/month

_____

4. Car loan payment

_____

$207/month

_____

5. College loan payment

_____

$30/month

_____

E. Answer these questions.

1. What bills do you pay every month?

_____

2. What bills are the same every month?

_____

3. What bills change every month?

_____

4. How can you save money?

_____

5. Are you saving money now?

_____

F. Read about Althea's additional expenses.

Althea pays some bills once a month, for example, her rent, electric, gas, and water bills. She pays some bills once every two months, for example, her water bill. Althea pays her car insurance twice a year. In March she pays $375. From April to September she saves $62.50 a month. So in September, she has $375 to pay her car insurance bill. Althea pays her rental insurance once a year in April. Every month she saves $11. So in April, she has $132 to pay her rental insurance.

What expenses does Althea have once a month? Once every two months? Once a year? Twice a year?

 # Problem Solving

Making a Budget

Make a budget for Althea. Write down her expenses.

EXPENSES	AMOUNT PER MONTH
Rent	$500
Food	$200
Rental insurance	
Gas for her car	
Car insurance	
Electricity	
Gas	
Water	
Telephone	
Car loan payment	
College loan payment	
OTHER EXPENSES	
TOTAL EXPENSES	

Althea's take-home pay:
$762.50/two weeks x 2 =

Now, make a budget for yourself. Write down your expenses. How much do you spend a month for rent, food, electricity, and other necessities?

 **Grammar**

Can, Want, and Need + to + Verb

A. Read some more about Althea.

> Althea needs to save money. She needs four new tires for her car. They cost about $160. She needs to buy them within three months She's saving money for them.
>   Althea wants to save money; she wants to buy a new TV. She wants a color TV, but color TV's are expensive. She's going to save her money for a long time. She's going to save money for a color TV.

How can Althea save money? Give her suggestions. Use *can.* Follow the example.

Example: Althea eats lunch at a restaurant at least twice a week.

She can take her lunch.

She can eat at a restaurant only once a week.

1. Althea goes to the movies twice a month.

_____ go only once a month.

_____ go in the afternoon. It's cheaper then.

2. Althea drives to work every day. It costs her $15 a week for gas and $7.50 a week for parking.

She can _____

She can _____

3. Althea goes hiking in the country twice a month. She drives about 200 miles each time.

She can _____

She can _____

4. Althea makes long-distance calls to her parents and friends every week.

She can _____

She can _____

5. Althea likes to buy books. She buys a new book every week.

She can _____

She can _____

6. Althea has her own apartment. The rent is $500 a month.

She can _____

She can _____

B. Quan and Mayling are having a baby. They're saving for the baby. They need to buy a washing machine and a dryer. Answer the questions about Quan and Mayling. Follow the example.

Example: Quan and Mayling usually go to the movies every Saturday night. But they want to save money. It's a Saturday night. What are they doing?

_They're watching TV._____

1. Quan and Mayling usually eat at a restaurant every Friday night. But they want to save money. It's Friday night. What are they doing?

_____

2. Quan likes to have steak once a week for dinner. But steak is expensive, and Quan and Mayling want to save money. What are they eating for dinner tonight?

_____

3. Quan and Mayling like to go to a baseball game about two or three times a month during the summer. Tonight there's a baseball game. But the tickets are expensive, and Quan and Mayling want to save money. What are Quan and Mayling doing?

_____

C. Form questions with the following phrases. Answer them. Use the present tense. Follow the example.

Example: pay your rent   (when)

_When do you pay your rent?_____

_I pay my rent on the first day of every month._____

1. Pay your telephone bill   (when)

_____

_____

2. spend a week on food   (how much)

_____

_____

3. need to buy this year   (what)

_____

_____

4. want to buy this year   (what)

_____

_____

5. save a month   (how much)

_____

_____

D. Complete these conversations. Follow the example.

Example: Charlie I can't save money.

           Nilda You need to _make a budget._ _____

1. Mayling We need to save money for the baby.

   Quan We can _____

2.   Jane Let's go out to lunch today.

   Althea No, _____

3.   Althea I always need to paint or fix my apartment.

   Jane _____

4.   Althea _____

   Jane You need to save money for a long time.

5. Mayling Let's go to the movies tonight.

   Quan No, _____

Reading

Do you want to save money? You can make a budget and save money. It's important to know how much money you spend a month. Some expenses are the same every month, for example, rent, car loan payments, and car insurance. But some expenses change every month. For example, let's say during the winter you use a lot of gas to heat your home. Then your gas bill is very high. In the summer you don't heat your home. Then your gas bill is low. You spend a different amount each month on gas for your home.

You can average your expenses. For example, let's say in June you spend $60 for gas for your car. In July you spend $55. In August you take a trip during the weekend. You spend $100 for gas for your car in August.

June	$ 60	
July	55	
August	100	
	$215	$215 ÷ 3 = $71.67

You spend an average of $71.67 a month for gas for your car for these three months.

It's important to save money for emergencies. Let's say you and your husband or wife work. Your husband or wife has an accident and can't work for two months. What can you do? How can you pay your bills? You can save money every month for emergencies. It's important to include money for emergencies in your budget.

■ Comprehension Questions

Write the answers to the following questions.

1. How can you save money?

   _____

2. Which expenses are the same every month?

   _____

3. Which expenses change every month?

   _____

4. Why is it important to average your expenses?

   _____

5. What are some possible emergencies?

   _____

6. Do you have money for emergencies?

_____

 # Listening Comprehension

A. Fill in the blanks with the amounts that your teacher says. Remember to use the dollar sign.

Quan and Mayling want to make a budget. Quan's an architect. His take-home pay is

_____ a month. Mayling works at a university. Her take-home pay is _____ a

month. Their house payment is _____ a month. They have home insurance. It costs

_____ a year. Taxes on their house cost _____ a year. Their gas, electric, and

water bills are about _____ a month. The telephone is about _____ a month.

Quan drives to work. Gas costs about _____ a week. Parking costs _____ a

week. Mayling takes the bus. She spends _____ a week. They have car insurance. It

costs about _____ a year. Their car loan payment is _____ a month. Repairs on

their car cost about _____ a year. Quan and Mayling spend about _____ a week

on food. Their medical expenses are about _____ a year.

Quan likes to buy clothes. He spends about _____ a month on clothes. Mayling

likes to go to the movies every week. The movies cost _____ a week.

B. Listen to the story above again. Answer these questions.

1. What other expenses do Quan and Mayling have?

_____

_____

2. Quan and Mayling are having a baby. They want to save money for the baby. How much
can they save each week?

_____

Problem Solving

Making a Budget

Make a budget for Quan and Mayling based on the information in the Listening Comprehension exercises. What other expenses do Quan and Mayling have? How much can they save each month?

EXPENSES	AMOUNT PER MONTH
House payment	
Home insurance	
House taxes	
Gas, electricity, water	
Telephone	
Gas for their car	
Parking	
Bus	
Car insurance	
Car loan payment	
Car repairs	
Food	
Medical expenses	
Clothes	
Movies	
OTHER EXPENSES	
TOTAL EXPENSES	
Quan's take-home pay	
Mayling's take-home pay	
TOTAL TAKE-HOME PAY	

 **Problem Solving**

Meeting Expenses

Work in groups to solve these problems. Write down your answers. Discuss your answers with the rest of the class.

1. Quan and Mayling are having a baby. They want to buy a washing machine and dryer soon. How can they save money? How can they decrease their expenses?

   _____

   _____

   _____

   _____

2. Let's say Quan and Mayling's refrigerator stops working. It costs $150 to repair it or $500 to buy a new one. How can they save money? How can they decrease their expenses?

   _____

   _____

   _____

   _____

3. Let's say after Quan and Mayling have their baby, Mayling doesn't want to work. She wants to stay home with the baby for a year. Can they pay their bills?

   _____

   _____

   _____

   _____

4. Quan and Mayling want to save money for their child's education. How much can they save a month?

   _____

   _____

   _____

Banking– Savings Accounts

 Learner Objectives

Consumer Competencies
• Becoming familiar with and being able to use banking services, such as, savings accounts

Grammatical Structures
• Being able to understand and use the following structures: the past tense and *should*

Vocabulary Items
• Being able to understand and use the following words in context:

Nouns		Verbs	Adjectives
account	interest	check	convenient
bank manager	interest rate	deposit	minimum
bill	loan	earn	
auto mechanic	paycheck	fix	
change	robber	insure	
checking account	savings account	lose	
clerk	savings and loan	print	
credit card	association	repair	
coin	signature card	rob	
department store	social security number	save	
deposit	withdrawal slip	sign	
deposit slip		withdraw	

17

 # Dialogue

Charlie and Nilda are going to get married soon. They're reading the Sunday newspaper. Nilda's looking at the department store ads.

Nilda	Charlie, look at these towels. Aren't they beautiful!
Charlie	Yes, they're nice, but expensive.
Nilda	I want to buy so many things for our apartment—sheets, towels, furniture, dishes.
Charlie	We need a lot of things. We should start saving money.
Nilda	Maybe we should open a savings account together. Look, Charlie, here's an ad for a bank.
Charlie	Let's see. Nilda, we can open a savings account with just $50. But this bank is on the other side of town. We should open a savings account at a bank nearby. We can call a few banks tomorrow and ask about savings accounts.

■ Comprehension Questions

1. What are Charlie and Nilda doing?

   _____

2. What's Nilda looking at?

   _____

3. What does Nilda want to buy?

   _____

4. What should Charlie and Nilda do to save money?

   _____

5. Where's the bank?

   _____

6. Where should they open a savings account?

   _____

7. What are Charlie and Nilda going to do?

 # Reading

Charlie and Nilda decided to open a savings account at Fidelity Bank. Fidelity Bank is convenient for them because it's near Charlie's apartment. It's open late on Fridays, so they can go there after work.

Yesterday, they went to the bank. They asked the bank manager about savings accounts. They decided to open a savings account. That means they can deposit (put in) or withdraw (take out) their money any time. First they signed a signature card. The signature card shows the bank how they sign their names. On the signature card they printed their names, addresses, home phone numbers, social security numbers, driver's license numbers, dates of birth, occupations, and their employers' names and addresses. Charlie and Nilda deposited $200. The bank manager gave them their account number for their new savings account.

Fidelity Bank pays 1.75% interest on savings accounts. It pays interest every day. That means Charlie and Nilda can deposit or withdraw money any time, and they don't lose interest. Every time Charlie and Nilda deposit money in their savings account or withdraw money from their savings account, they need their account number.

■ Comprehension Questions

Write the answers to the following questions.

1. Where did Charlie and Nilda decide to open an account? Why?

2. What kind of account did they open? Why?

3. What did they do first?

4. What's a signature card?

5. What did they write on the signature card?

_____

6. How much money did they deposit?

_____

7. What did the bank manager give to Charlie and Nilda?

_____

8. How much interest does Fidelity Bank pay on savings accounts?

_____

9. How often does the bank pay interest?

_____

10. What do Charlie and Nilda need when they deposit or withdraw money?

_____

 # Problem Solving

Signature Cards

This is the signature card Charlie and Nilda filled out to open their savings account.

Welcome to Fidelity Bank!
To open your Fidelity Bank account, please complete and sign below.

Please print:

NAME *Charles Wisnick* HOME PHONE *555-2368*

HOME ADDRESS *412 40th St., Pittsburgh, PA 15222*

SOCIAL SECURITY NO. *659-12-3450* DRIVER'S LICENSE NO. *W126-4388-764* DATE OF BIRTH *2/24/73*

OCCUPATION *auto mechanic* EMPLOYER *Joe's Garage*

EMPLOYER'S ADDRESS *14 Theodore Ave., Pittsburgh, PA 15226*

If this is a Joint Account, complete the following:

JOINT ACCOUNT NAME *Nilda S. Ramos* HOME PHONE *555·4592*

HOME ADDRESS *5822 College Ave, Pittsburgh PA 15223*

SOCIAL SECURITY NO. *256·68·2364* DRIVER'S LICENSE NO. *R267·3268·461* DATE OF BIRTH *3/14/75*

OCCUPATION *bookkeeper* EMPLOYER *Exact Accounting, Inc.*

EMPLOYER'S ADDRESS *236 36th St., Pittsburgh, PA 15223*

Please sign here:

SIGNATURE *Charles Wisnick*

JOINT ACCOUNT SIGNATURE *Nilda S. Ramos*

Depositor(s) signing above acknowledge(s) receipt of and agree(s) to the Rules and Regulations of the Bank for the account, including but not limited to the Depositor's Agreement contained within Fidelity Bank's Welcome Brochure.

Under penalties of perjury, I certify (1) that the number shown on this card is my correct social security number and (2) that I am not subject to backup withholding either because I have not been notified that I am subject to backup withholding as a result of a failure to report all interest or dividends, or the Internal Revenue Service has notified me that I am no longer subject to backup withholding. (Instruction to signer: If you have been notified by the IRS that you are subject to backup withholding due to notified payee underreporting and you have not been notified that the backup withholding is terminated, you must strike out the language in clause 2 above.)

SIGNATURE *Charles Wisnick* DATE *5/24/96*

Now, fill out a signature card to open an individual savings account.

Welcome to Fidelity Bank!

To open your Fidelity Bank account, please complete and sign below.

Please print:

NAME _____ HOME PHONE _____

HOME ADDRESS _____

SOCIAL SECURITY NO. _____ DRIVER'S LICENSE NO. _____ DATE OF BIRTH _____

OCCUPATION _____ EMPLOYER _____

EMPLOYER'S ADDRESS _____

If this is a Joint Account, complete the following:

JOINT ACCOUNT NAME _____ HOME PHONE _____

HOME ADDRESS _____

SOCIAL SECURITY NO. _____ DRIVER'S LICENSE NO. _____ DATE OF BIRTH _____

OCCUPATION _____ EMPLOYER _____

EMPLOYER'S ADDRESS _____

Please sign here:

SIGNATURE _____

JOINT ACCOUNT SIGNATURE _____

Depositor(s) signing above acknowledge(s) receipt of and agree(s) to the Rules and Regulations of the Bank for the account, including but not limited to the Depositor's Agreement contained within Fidelity Bank's Welcome Brochure.

Under penalties of perjury, I certify (1) that the number shown on this card is my correct social security number and (2) that I am not subject to backup withholding either because I have not been notified that I am subject to backup withholding as a result of a failure to report all interest or dividends, or the Internal Revenue Service has notified me that I am no longer subject to backup withholding. (Instruction to signer: If you have been notified by the IRS that you are subject to backup withholding due to notified payee underreporting and you have not been notified that the backup withholding is terminated, you must strike out the language in clause 2 above.)

SIGNATURE _____ DATE _____

Problem Solving

Withdrawal/Deposit Slips

Charlie and Nilda decide to deposit more money in their savings account. They deposit a $25 check and $10 in cash.

SAVINGS Withdrawal		Deposit		
NAME Charlie Wisnick		CURRENCY	10	00
		COIN		
ACCOUNT NO. 939-5257910		CHECKS LIST SINGLY	25	00
DATE 19 $				
DOLLARS				
SIGNATURE		TOTAL	35	00
ALL ITEMS ARE ACCEPTED SUBJECT TO THIS FINANCIAL INSTITUTION'S RULES AND REGULATIONS PERTAINING TO SAVINGS ACCOUNTS.		LESS CASH RECEIVED	—	
Fidelity Bank of Pittsburgh, PA		NET DEPOSIT	35	00

⑈8989 20088⑈

This is what their savings account statement looks like. Fidelity Bank sends a statement to them every month.

FIDELITY BANK
of Pittsburgh, PA

```
NAME(S):  CHARLES WISNICK        ACCOUNT:  939-5257910
          NILDA S. RAMOS
ADDRESS:  412 40TH STREET        DATE:     06/15/96
          PITTSBURGH, PA 15222

-----------------------------------------------------------------
BEGINNING BALANCE:  05/24/96   $200.00  (NEW ACCOUNT)
ENDING BALANCE:     06/15/96   $235.00
-----------------------------------------------------------------
        DEPOSITS                          WITHDRAWALS

    DATE      AMOUNT               DATE      AMOUNT
  05/24/96    $200.00
  05/30/96     $35.00
```

Mayling withdrew $13.50 from her savings account. Fill out the withdrawal slip for her.

SAVINGS	Withdrawal		Deposit		
			CURRENCY		
NAME			COIN		
ACCOUNT NO.			CHECKS LIST SINGLY		
DATE 19 $					
	DOLLARS				
SIGNATURE			TOTAL		
ALL ITEMS ARE ACCEPTED SUBJECT TO THIS FINANCIAL INSTITUTION'S RULES AND REGULATIONS PERTAINING TO SAVINGS ACCOUNTS.			LESS CASH RECEIVED		
Fidelity Bank of Pittsburgh, PA			NET DEPOSIT		

⑈8989 20088⑈

 # Grammar

Past Tense

One way to form the past tense is to add *ed* to the simple form of regular verbs. If the simple form ends in *e,* we add only *d* (smoke → smoked).

I work*ed* yesterday.	We work*ed* yesterday.
You work*ed* yesterday.	You work*ed* yesterday.
He, she, it, work*ed* yesterday.	They work*ed* yesterday.

We use *did* in affirmative questions and affirmative short answers to show past time. We use the simple form of the verb after *did* in affirmative questions.

Question Form

Did	Subject	Verb (simple form)	Complement
Did	Charlie	work	yesterday?
Did	you	go	yesterday?

Short Answer

Yes, he did.
Yes, I did.

In negative questions, negative statements, and negative short answers we use *didn't* (*did* + *not*). We use the simple form of the verb after *didn't*, except in short answers.

Question Form

Didn't Did + Not	Subject	Verb (simple form)	Complement
Didn't	Charlie	work	yesterday?

Short Answer

No, he didn't.

Statement Form

Subject	Didn't Did + not	Verb (simple form)	Complement
Charlie	didn't	work	yesterday.

We use these expressions to show past time:

last night, last week, last month, last year, last Sunday;
three days ago, two years ago, a week ago;
yesterday, yesterday morning, yesterday afternoon, yesterday evening.

Irregular Verbs

Many common verbs are irregular in the past tense. These are used in this unit:

Simple present tense	Past tense		Simple present tense	Past tense
be	was, were		make	made
buy	bought		pay	paid
catch	caught		read	read
get	got		spend	spent
give	gave		withdraw	withdrew
go	went		write	wrote
have	had			

Note the past tense of the verb *be:*

I was	we were
you were	you were
he, she, it was	they were

Question Form

Were you at the game yesterday?
Wasn't he sick yesterday?

Short Answer

Yes, I was.
No, he wasn't.

■ Exercises

A. Fill in the blanks with the past tense form of the verb. Follow the example.

Example: The Consumer Education class _discussed_____ (discuss) banking.

1. We _____ (open) a savings account two months ago.

2. Quan and Mayling _____ (save) $50 last month.

3. You _____ (wash) the dishes after dinner last night.

4. The Consumer Education class _____ (talk) about budgets last week.

5. I _____ (ask) the bank manager about savings accounts.

B. Fill in the blanks with the past tense form of the verb. These verbs are irregular. Follow the example.

Example: I _withdrew_____ (withdraw) $50 from my savings account two days ago.

1. Quan and Mayling _____ (make) a budget last week.

2. They _____ (write) down their expenses yesterday morning.

3. Quan and Mayling _____ (spend) $12 a week last year for the movies.

4. The bank _____ (pay) 1.75% interest last year on savings accounts.

5. You _____ (get) a package in the mail yesterday.

C. Form *yes/no* questions in the past tense. Answer them with a short answer. Follow the example.

Example: _Did the students talk_____ (the students/talk) about banking last week?

_Yes, they did._____

1. _____ (you/go) shopping this morning?

   _____

2. _____ (Quan and Mayling/need) to save money last year?

   _____

3. _____ (we/receive) any mail yesterday?

   _____

4. _____ (you/fill) out a signature card to open a savings
   account?

   _____

5. _____ (Charlie and Nilda/deposit) $200 in their savings
   account last week?

   _____

D. Form questions in the past tense. Answer them. Follow the example.

Example: Where _did Charlie and Nilda go_ (Charlie and Nilda/go) Friday after work?

   They went to the bank. _____

1. Why _____ (you/need) to save money last year?

   _____

2. Why _____ (you/decide) to open a savings account?

   _____

3. Where _____ (you/open) a bank account?

   _____

4. How much interest _____ (your bank/pay) on savings accounts
   last year?

   _____

5. When _____ (you/deposit) your paycheck in your bank account?

   _____

E. This is what Mr. Wilson did in the evenings last week. Answer the questions according to the example.

Sunday	Monday	Tuesday	Wednesday
stay home	play tennis	teach the Consumer Education class	watch TV

Thursday	Friday	Saturday
teach the Consumer Education class	go to a baseball game	go to the movies

Example: Did Mr. Wilson eat dinner at a restaurant Sunday evening?

No, he didn't. He stayed home.

1. Did Mr. Wilson read a book Monday evening?

_____

2. Did Mr. Wilson go to the movies Tuesday evening?

_____

3. Did Mr. Wilson teach the Consumer Education class Wednesday evening?

_____

4. Did Mr. Wilson wash his car Thursday evening?

_____

5. Did Mr. Wilson go to a party Friday evening?

_____

6. Did Mr. Wilson go bowling Saturday evening?

_____

F. Form *yes/no* questions in the past tense with the following phrases. Answer them. Follow the example.

Example: pay the telephone bill

Did you pay the telephone bill last month?

No, I didn't.

1. open a savings account

_____

_____

2. make a budget

_____

_____

3. save money for emergencies

_____

_____

4. go to class

_____

_____

5. deposit money in your savings account

_____

_____

G. Form questions in the past tense with the following phrases. Answer them. Follow the example.

Example: pay the telephone bill (when)

When did you pay the telephone bill?

I paid it yesterday.

1. withdraw $65 (why)

_____

_____

2. go shopping (when)

_____

_____

3. go last night (where)

_____

_____

4. make a budget (why)

_____

_____

5. buy a new shirt (when)

_____

_____

H. Rewrite this story in the past tense.

Denise gets an invitation to a wedding. She knows how much she can afford to spend for everything she needs. She needs to buy a dress, shoes, and a purse. She also wants to buy a really nice gift for the bride and groom.

She makes a budget. She wants to make sure she has enough money left to buy the gift after she pays for her clothing.

After she finishes work, she goes shopping for the clothes. She goes to a few different stores until she finds a dress, shoes, and purse at prices she can afford.

She goes shopping for the gift the next day. Denise is happy because she bought everything she needs.

I. This is a typical day for Mayling.

Mayling's a university professor. She works five days a week. Sometimes, she works on the weekend. She has a class at 10 A.M. She goes to lunch at 12:30 P.M. Sometimes, she goes to a restaurant with other professors or students. She buys a sandwich. In the afternoon, she prepares for her classes. She usually goes home about 4:30 P.M.

This is a typical day for Charlie.

Charlie's an auto mechanic. He works five days a week. He goes to work at 7:30 A.M. He starts work at 8:00. He repairs autos all day. He fixes motors. He changes tires. He gets a coffee break at 10:30. He has lunch at noon. He goes home at 5 P.M. When he gets home, he washes his face and hands and then has dinner. In the evening, he watches TV or goes out with Nilda.

Yesterday was a typical day for Mayling and a typical day for Charlie. Tell the class what they did.

Now, tell the class what you do on a typical day. Tell the class what you did yesterday.

J. Here is some information about Althea. Talk about Althea. Talk about her education and experience.

Althea		
Education	Central High School	1981–1985
	University of Pittsburgh, B.A., Spanish	1985–1989
Travel	Mexico	6 months, 1989
Employment	waitress	summers, 1986, 1987
	recreation counselor, city park program	summers, 1988, 1989
	office worker	part-time, 1990–1991
	travel agent	1991–present

Now, make a chart about yourself and the other students in the class. Talk about your education and experience.

K. Complete these conversations in the past tense.

1. Did you open _____
at People's Savings and Loan Association?

No, _____

2. What time _____ yesterday?

8 o'clock.

3. How much _____

$75.

4. _____

We had hamburgers, French fries, and soft drinks.

5. Did you go to class last night?

No, _____

 **Grammar**

Should

Should usually refers to the present or future. It is followed by the simple form of the verb.

Should expresses a suggestion. In the affirmative it means that it is advisable to do something. For example, *The students should do their homework.*

Shouldn't means that it is advisable *not* to do something. For example, *You shouldn't spend so much money.*

Questions with *should* are used to ask for advice or suggestions. For example, *Should I open an account at First National Bank or at Fidelity Bank?*

	Subject	Should	Verb (simple form)	Complement
Affirmative	Charlie	should	open	a savings account.
Negative	Charlie	should not shouldn't	keep	his money at home.

	Should	Subject	Verb (simple form)	Complement
Question Form	Should	Nilda	open	a savings account?

Short Answer

Yes, she should.
No, she shouldn't.

■ Exercises

A. Read the following dialogue. Althea is talking to her friend José who is from Ecuador.

Althea	Hi, José. How are you?
José	Terrible.
Althea	What's wrong?
José	Someone robbed my apartment last week. The robber took $350.
Althea	Oh, no! Did you call the police?
José	No.
Althea	Why not?
José	My English isn't very good. I didn't know what to say to them.
Althea	I'm going to give you some advice, José. If this happens again, you should call the police immediately. You should try to remember everything. You should explain everything to the police.

José	That's difficult for a foreigner.
Althea	Then, you should ask me to help you. Do you always keep your money at home?
José	Yes, I keep it in a box in my bedroom.
Althea	Oh, no! José, you should open a savings account. You shouldn't keep your money at home. Let's go to the bank right now.

B. Answer these questions based on the dialogue.

1. What happened to José last week?

_____

2. How much did the robber take?

_____

3. Did José call the police? Why not?

_____

C. Answer these questions with short answers. Refer to the dialogue.

1. Should José call the police?

_____

2. Should he explain everything to the police?

_____

3. Should he ask Althea to help him?

_____

4. Should he keep his money at home?

_____

5. Should he go to the bank to find out about savings accounts?

_____

6. Should he open a savings account?

_____

D. Fill in the blanks with *should* and the verb. Follow the example.

Example: José <u>should open</u> (open) a savings account.

1. Before you open a savings account, you _____ (call) several banks and savings and loan associations.

2. You _____ (ask) for information about savings accounts because there are many different plans for saving.

3. You _____ (find) out the interest rates.

4. You _____ (save) money for emergencies.

5. You _____ (make) a budget.

E. Fill in the blanks with *shouldn't* and the verb.

Example: José <u>shouldn't keep</u> (keep) a lot of money at home.

1. You _____ (be) late for work.

2. Nilda _____ (spend) all her money.

3. Althea _____ (pay) her bills late.

4. José _____ (carry) a lot of cash in his pocket.

5. You _____ (forget) your account number when you go to the bank.

F. Form *yes/no* questions with *should* and the following phrases. Write a short answer. Follow the example.

Example: open a savings account

<u>Should Charlie and Nilda open a savings account?</u>

<u>Yes, they should.</u>

1. save money

_____

_____

2. buy a new auto

_____

_____

3. take an umbrella

_____

_____

4. go to the doctor

_____

_____

5. come to class on time

_____

_____

G. Complete these conversations. Use *should,* if possible.

Example: <u>Should we open an account</u> at First National Bank or Fidelity Bank?

<u>Fidelity Bank. It's close to our house.</u>

1. How much _____ in our savings account?

_____

2. I have a terrible headache!

You should _____

3. What time _____

Come at 2:00.

4. Oh, no! I gained two pounds!

_____

5. _____

I should do it, but I don't want to.

H. Give advice about the following situations. Use *should* or *shouldn't*.

Example: José keeps his money under the bed.

<u>He should open a bank account.</u>

<u>He shouldn't keep his money at home.</u>

1. Someone robbed José's apartment.

_____

_____

2. Nilda and Charlie want to save money.

_____

_____

3. It's cold outside.

_____

_____

4. The phone is ringing.

_____

_____

5. My clothes are dirty.

_____

_____

Listening Comprehension

A. Listen to your teacher. Write the numbers that you hear.

1. _____ _____ _____ _____ _____ _____ _____ _____

How much did Althea withdraw? _____

2. _____ _____ _____ _____ _____ _____ _____ _____

How much did Althea withdraw? _____

3. _____ _____ _____ _____ _____ _____ _____ _____

How much did Althea withdraw? _____

4. _____ _____ _____ _____ _____ _____ _____ _____

How much did Althea withdraw? _____

5. _____ _____ _____ _____ _____ _____ _____ _____

How much did Althea withdraw? _____

B. Listen to your teacher. Write the numbers that you hear.

1. Mr. Wilson's at a department store. He's buying a pair of pants. They cost _____.

He gives the clerk _____. The clerk is counting the change. Write the numbers

that you hear.

_____ _____ _____ _____

How much change did the clerk give Mr. Wilson? _____

What coins and bills did the clerk give Mr. Wilson? _____

_____

2. Quan's at a fast-food restaurant. He gets a hamburger, French fries, and a chocolate

milkshake. They cost _____. He gives the clerk _____. The clerk is counting

his change. Write the numbers that you hear.

_____ _____ _____ _____

How much change did the clerk give Quan? _____

What coins did the clerk give Quan? _____

_____

3. Mayling's at the supermarket. Her food costs _____. Mayling gives the

clerk _____. The clerk is counting her change. Write the numbers that you hear.

_____ _____ _____ _____ _____ _____ _____

How much change did the clerk give Mayling? _____

What coins and bills did the clerk give Mayling? _____

_____

 # Reading

Choosing a Bank or Savings and Loan Association

In the Consumer Education class the students read the following information about choosing a bank or savings and loan association.

You should choose a bank or savings and loan association very carefully. You should check many things before you open a bank account. Here are some things you should look for:

Location   You should be sure the bank or savings and loan association is convenient. It should be near your house or your job.

Hours   You should be sure the bank or savings and loan association is open when you can go there. For example, let's say you work from 8 A.M. to 5 P.M. You should find a bank or savings and loan association near your home that's open on Saturdays or after 5 P.M. during the week. Or you should find a bank or savings and loan association near your job. Then you can go during your lunch hour.

Services
Savings Accounts
Banks and savings and loan associations have different types of savings plans and pay interest in different ways. Savings and loan associations usually pay more interest than banks. You should check the interest rate on the different savings plans. Compare these two plans:

The interest rate for savings accounts at First National Bank is 1.75%. First National Bank pays interest every six months. Let's say, you open a savings account on January 2 and deposit $500. On March 30, you withdraw $200. On June 30, the First National Bank pays you interest on $300. It doesn't pay you interest on the $200 because you withdrew it before June 30. On June 30, you have $300 and $2.63 interest.

The interest rate for savings accounts at People's Savings and Loan Association is 1.9%. People's Savings and Loan Association pays interest every six months. Let's say you open a savings account on January 2 and deposit $500. On March 30, you withdraw $200. On June 30, People's Savings and Loan Association pays you interest on $300. It doesn't pay you interest on the $200 because you withdrew it before June 30. On June 30, you have $300 and $2.85 interest.

Checking Accounts

Banks offer checking accounts; savings and loan associations usually do not. A checking account is a safe way to pay your bills, rent, etc. You put money in your account. You write checks to a person or place to spend the money in your checking account. The check tells the bank to pay a specific amount of money from your account to the person or place.

Loans

Both banks and savings and loan associations offer loans.

Credit Cards

Banks offer credit cards; savings and loan associations usually do not.

You should be sure the bank is a member of the Federal Deposit Insurance Corporation (F.D.I.C.) and the savings and loan association a member of the Federal Savings and Loan Insurance Corporation (F.S.L.I.C.). The F.D.I.C. and the F.S.L.I.C. insure your money. This means if there's a fire or if someone robs the bank, you do not lose your money.

■ Comprehension Questions

Write the answers to the following questions.

1. Why should the bank or savings and loan association be near your job or house?

   _____

   _____

2. Does a bank or a savings and loan association usually pay more interest on savings accounts?

   _____

   _____

3. How often does First National Bank pay interest? How often does People's Savings and Loan Association pay interest? Do you prefer First National Bank's plan for savings accounts or People's Savings and Loan Association's plan for savings accounts? Why?

   _____

   _____

4. What is a checking account?

_____

_____

5. What services do banks offer? What services do savings and loan associations offer?

_____

_____

6. Why should a bank be a member of the F.D.I.C. and a savings and loan association a member of the F.S.L.I.C.?

_____

_____

 Problem Solving

Compare First National Bank and People's Savings and Loan Association. Where should you open a savings account? Which place is better for you? Why?

	First National Bank	People's Savings and Loan Association
Location	near your home	near your job
Hours	Monday – Friday 9 A.M. – 3 P.M.	Monday – Thursday 9 A.M. – 3 P.M.
	Saturday 9 A.M. – noon	Friday 9 A.M. – 6 P.M.
Interest Rates (on savings accounts)	1.75% paid every 6 months	1.9% paid every 6 months
Other Services	checking accounts, loans, credit cards	loans
	member F.D.I.C.	member F.S.L.I.C.

Banking–Checking Accounts

 Learner Objectives

Consumer Competencies

- Becoming familiar with and being able to use banking services, for example, checking accounts and credit cards
- Beginning to develop an understanding of the basic principles of credit systems

Grammatical Structures

- Being able to understand and use the following structures: the past continuous tense and *must* and *have to*

Vocabulary Items

- Being able to understand and use the following words in context:

Nouns		Verbs	Adjective
automated teller machine	identification	afford	canceled
balance	purchase	apply	
bank statement	receipt	bounce	
billing date	record	cash	
cash	service charge	charge	
charge form	teller	deduct	
check	vending machine	disappear	
checkbook		endorse	
customer		fill out	
		run into	

41

 # Dialogue

Yesterday, Nilda and Charlie were walking in the park when suddenly…

Nilda	Oh, no! Charlie, where's my purse?
Charlie	Don't you have it?
Nilda	I did, but it disappeared!
Charlie	Nilda, purses don't just disappear. Think carefully. When did you have it last?
Nilda	I had it when I left the house…I had it when we stopped to get a hot dog.
Charlie	OK. Let's go back to the hot dog stand.

(*They find the purse at the hot dog stand.*)

Nilda	(*Looking in her wallet*) Thank goodness. It's still here. I was really worried.
Charlie	Nilda, why are you carrying so much money?
Nilda	It's from my paycheck. I cashed it today.
Charlie	You're carrying your whole paycheck in your purse? Why didn't you deposit it in your checking account?
Nilda	I don't have a checking account. I don't know anything about checking accounts.
Charlie	Nilda, you have to open an account. It's not safe to carry all that cash. Do it tomorrow.

■ Comprehension Questions

1. What happened when Nilda and Charlie were walking in the park?

   _____

2. Where did Nilda leave her purse?

   _____

3. Was her money still in her purse?

   _____

4. How much money was Nilda carrying in her purse?

   _____

5. Why was she carrying so much money?

   _____

6. Why didn't Nilda deposit her paycheck in her checking account?

_____

7. What did Charlie tell her to do? Why?

_____

 # Grammar

Past Continuous Tense

We form the past continuous tense with the past tense of the verb *be* (*was, were*) and the *ing*-form of the verb (*talking, running, sleeping*).

Affirmative

Subject	Be	V + *ing*	Complement
Charlie and Nilda	were	walking	in the park yesterday afternoon.

Negative

Subject	Be	V + *ing*	Complement
Charlie	wasn't	reading	a book yesterday afternoon.

Question Form

Be	Subject	V + *ing*	Complement
Were	Charlie and Nilda	walking	in the park yesterday afternoon?
Where were	Charlie and Nilda	walking	yesterday afternoon?

Short Answer

Yes, they were.
No, they weren't.

We use the past continuous tense to describe a continuing action at a specific time in the past:

I was reading a book yesterday afternoon.

We also use the past continuous tense with *when* and the past tense to describe two past actions.

In the following sentences, which action came first?

> Nilda and Charlie were walking in the park when it started to rain.
> When it started to rain, Nilda and Charlie were walking in the park.

The sudden action "it started to rain" interrupts, or comes after, the continuous action "Nilda and Charlie were walking in the park."

Now, compare the following sentences:

> What were you doing when the fire began?
> I was sleeping.

> What did you do when the fire began?
> I called the fire department.

In the first pair of sentences, the fire began after the subject began sleeping; in the second pair, first the fire began and then the subject called the fire department.

■ Exercises

A. Tell what Quan was doing yesterday. Follow the example.

Example:

7 A.M.
Sleep

At 7 A.M., Quan was sleeping.

8 A.M.	10 A.M.	10:30 A.M.	12:30 P.M.
Eat breakfast	Cut the grass	Talk to his neighbor	Eat lunch

2 P.M.	6:30 P.M.	8 P.M.
Swim	Take a shower	Eat dinner at a restaurant

Now, tell what you were doing at these times yesterday.

B. Here's what Mr. Wilson was doing yesterday at different times in the day. Answer the questions. Follow the example.

8 A.M.	10 A.M.	Noon	4 P.M.
Sleep	Eat breakfast	Play tennis	Walk in the park

6 P.M.	8:30 P.M.
Eat dinner	Watch TV

Example: Was Mr. Wilson eating breakfast at 8 A.M.?

<u>No, he wasn't. He was sleeping.</u>

1. Was Mr. Wilson cleaning his apartment at 10 A.M.?

   _____

2. Was Mr. Wilson eating lunch at noon?

   _____

3. Was Mr. Wilson taking a shower at 4 P.M.?

   _____

4. Was Mr. Wilson shopping at 6 P.M.?

   _____

5. Was Mr. Wilson dancing at a party at 8:30 P.M.?

   _____

C. Nilda went to the bank a few days ago. Tell what was happening when she entered the bank. Follow the example.

Example: Woman/deposit money

<u>When Nilda entered the bank, a woman was depositing money.</u>

1. Man/cash a check

   _____

2. Customers/wait in line

   _____

3. Man and woman/apply for a loan

   _____

4. Children/wait for their mother

   _____

5. Teller/talk to a customer

   _____

6. Woman/fill out a deposit slip

   _____

7. Guard/look out the window

   _____

8. Bank manager/talk on the phone

   _____

D. Fill in the blank with the correct form of the verb.

Example: The children _were walking_____ (walk) to school yesterday when it

   _began_____ (begin) to rain.

1. The Consumer Education class _____ (discuss) back accounts

   when Althea _____ (enter) the room.

2. When Charlie _____ (call), Nilda _____ (wash) her hair.

3. Althea _____ (shop) in the supermarket

   when she _____ (run) into Mr. Wilson.

4. Mayling _____ (wait) in line to vote

   when she _____ (meet) Quan.

5. The mailman _____ (deliver) letters

   when a dog _____ (bite) him.

E. Form questions with the subject and verb. Answer them. Follow the example.

Example: Where _were the children going_____ (children/go)

   when it _started_____ (start) to rain?

   _They were going to school._____

1. What _____ (bank manager/explain) to Nilda

   when his phone _____ (ring)?

   _____

2. Where _____ (Denise/go)

when she _____ (want) a dress?

_____

3. What _____ (Mr. Wilson/do)

when the lights _____ (go) out?

_____

4. What _____ (Charlie/dream) about

when his alarm clock _____ (ring)?

_____

5. When Nilda _____ (enter) the bank,

what _____ (teller/do)?

_____

F. Complete these conversations.

Example: What were you doing when I saw you this morning?

<u>I was waiting</u> _____ for the bus.

1. Who were you talking to when I saw you?

_____ to a friend.

2. _____

I was cashing a check.

3. _____ when the accident happened?

I was going to class.

4. _____

I was taking a shower.

5. _____ when the fire started?

_____

G. Combine the two sentences.

Example: Nilda was watching TV. Her father saw the ad for the Consumer Education class in the newspaper.

<u>Nilda was watching TV when her father saw the ad for the</u>

<u>Consumer Education class in the newspaper.</u>

1. Nilda's father was reading the newspaper. He saw the ad for the Consumer Education class.

_____

_____

2. Mayling was driving to the bank. It started to rain.

_____

_____

3. Nilda was filling out a signature card to open a checking account. Her pen ran out of ink.

_____

_____

4. Mr. Wilson was watching TV last night. His TV broke.

_____

_____

5. Quan and Mayling were living in New York. They fell in love.

_____

_____

H. Complete the questions. Answer them.

1. What were you doing when _____

_____

_____

2. Were you going to the bank when _____

_____

_____

3. Were you reading the newspaper when _____

_____

_____

4. Were you sleeping when _____

_____

_____

5. Where were you going when _____

_____

_____

I. Fill in the blanks with the correct form of the verb. Use the past tense or past continuous tense.

Nilda _____ (lose) her purse again. She finally _____

(decide) to open a checking account. She _____ (go) to the bank

yesterday. When she _____ (arrive), the bank manager

_____ (talk) to another customer. When the customer left, Nilda

_____ (ask) the bank manager for information about checking accounts.

Nilda _____ (fill) out the signature card when the phone

_____ (ring). When the bank manager finished talking on the phone,

Nilda _____ (give) him her paycheck to deposit in her new account.

    Nilda's checking account _____ (be) free, but she

_____ (pay) $11 for 200 checks. The bank is going to send her the

checks. The checks are going to have her name, address, and account number on them.

 **Dialogue**

The Consumer Education class is taking a break. The students are talking in the hall. Nilda wants to buy a candy bar from the vending machine.

Nilda	Oh, no, my purse! Where is it?
Charlie	Not again! Did you leave it in the classroom?
Nilda	Oh, yeah. Of course. That's where I left it.

(*Back in class*)

Nilda	Mr. Wilson, can we talk about checking accounts? I want to open one, but I need more information.
Althea	You don't have a checking account? How can you live without one? Everyone should have one. They're so convenient. You don't have to pay your bills in person. You just write a check and mail it. It saves gas and time, and it's safe.
Mr. Wilson	And your canceled checks are your receipts.
Nilda	What do you mean "canceled checks"?
Mr. Wilson	After you use your checks, the bank sends them back to you at the end of the month. That way, you have a record of the money you spent.
Althea	Yesterday, I was shopping, when I saw a dress that I really liked. It was perfect for work. I didn't have a lot of cash with me, so I wrote a check to pay for it.
Nilda	Do stores accept checks instead of cash?
Althea	Yes, but you have to have identification, like a driver's license or a credit card.
Nilda	Do banks charge for checking accounts?
Althea	Mine doesn't. I only have to pay for my checks. I think I pay about $11 for 200 checks.
Mayling	Our bank requires a minimum balance. We have to keep $50 in our account.
Mr. Wilson	Banks have a service charge. For example, some banks charge $3.75 a month and $.75 for every check you write. Other banks charge a once a month fee of $12. Nilda, you should check several banks to find the best plan for you.

■ **Comprehension Questions**

1. Why does Nilda need her purse?

_____

2. Where did she leave it?

_____

3. Why does Althea like checking accounts?

_____

4. What are "canceled checks"?

_____

5. Why did Althea use a check yesterday?

_____

6. What do you have to have to use a check in a store?

_____

7. Is there a charge for checking accounts?

_____

8. What are the advantages of a checking account?

_____

 # Grammar

Must/Have to

Must

Must is followed by the simple form of the verb. _Must_ refers to the present or future. _Must_ means that it is necessary to do something. It implies an obligation. For example, _You must stop your car at a red light._

    Must not means that it is necessary _not_ to do something. It is forbidden. For example, _we must not break the law._

	Subject	**Must**	**Verb (Simple form)**	**Complement**
**Affirmative**	You	must	sign	a signature card.
**Negative**	Children	must not	play	in the street.

Short Answer

Yes, you must.
No, you mustn't.

Have to

Must and *have to* generally express the same meaning in the affirmative, but *have to* is more common in conversations. *Must* occurs in formal speech and writing. *Have to* is usually used instead of *must* to ask a question, for example, *do I have to work today?*

In the negative, there is a difference in meaning between *must* and *have to*. *Must not* means that something is forbidden. *Don't have to* means that it is not necessary to do something. It expresses a lack of obligation. For example, *Friday is a holiday; I don't have to go to work.*

Affirmative	Nilda has to open a checking account.
	Quan and Mayling have to save money.
Negative	Children don't have to work.
Question Form	Do I have to go to school today?

Short Answer	Yes, you have to.	No, you don't have to.
	or	*or*
	Yes, you do.	No, you don't.

■ Exercises

A. Fill in the blank with *must* and the verb.

Example: Denise _must buy_____ (buy) a dress for the wedding.

1. Charlie and Nilda _____ (tell) the bank their social security numbers to open an account.

2. You _____ (sign) a signature card to open a savings or checking account.

3. Althea _____ (have) identification to use a check in a store.

4. You _____ (endorse) a check in order to cash it.

5. I _____ (pay) my rent every month.

B. Fill in the blank with *must not* and the verb.

Example: The sign says "No Smoking."

You _must not smoke_____ (smoke) here.

1. You _____ (stand) under a tree in a storm.

2. You _____ (drive) on the wrong side of the street.

3. Althea _____ (pay) her bills late.

4. You _____ (use) a pencil to write a check.

5. The sign says "Don't walk." You _____ (cross) the street.

C. Form *yes/no* questions with *have to* and the following phrases. Write a short answer in the affirmative or negative.

Example: go to the store

   Does Denise have to go to the store? _____

   Yes, she has to. _____

1. stop at a red light

_____

_____

2. answer the phone

_____

_____

3. pay bills on time

_____

_____

4. get up at 6 A.M.

_____

_____

5. use a pen to write a check

_____

_____

6. open a checking account

_____

_____

7. be on time

_____

_____

D. Complete these conversations. Use _must_ or _have to_.

Example: Charlie, <u>do I have to</u> _____ open a checking account? I don't need one.

<u>Yes, you do. You always lose your purse.</u> _____

1. Mom _____ go to school today?
Yes, you have to.

2. What _____ this afternoon?
I have to do my laundry.

3. Why _____ leave so early?

_____

4. _____ sign a signature card to open a bank account?

_____

5. _____ pay her bills in person?

No, _____

6. _____
No, you don't have you. You can do it tomorrow.

E. Answer the questions. Use _should, must,_ or _have to_.

1. Nilda has a check that she wants to deposit. It says "Pay to the order of Nilda S. Ramos." How should she endorse it? ("Endorse" means to sign her name on the back of the check.)

_____

2. The bank sends Althea her old checks with her bank statement. What should Althea do with them?

_____

3. Mr. Franco is always late. Today he's starting a new job. What does Mrs. Franco say to him?

_____

4. Charlie usually gets up at 5:30 A.M. to go to work. Tomorrow is a holiday. Why is he happy?

_____

5. You're going 75 mph on the highway. A police car is following you with the light flashing. What do you have to do?

_____

F. Give advice, suggestions, or make comments about the following situations. Use *should, have to,* or *must.*

Example: Mr. Franco is always late.

<u>Comment</u>: He should plan his time more carefully.

1. My friend's car is broken. I know how to fix it.

_____

2. Your apartment is on fire.

_____

3. The gas tank is almost empty.

_____

4. Althea needs money to buy a car.

_____

5. Your friend's going for an interview for a new job. His hair is dirty, and he's wearing blue jeans.

_____

6. Charlie has a toothache.

_____

7. My husband/wife wants to find a new job.

_____

8. Nilda endorsed her check before she arrived at the bank.

_____

9. Althea's writing a check for $50, but she only has $45 in her checking account.

_____

10. Your friend's writing a check. He's using a pencil.

_____

 # **Dialogue**

Althea is at home. She's opening the mail. Her friend Jane is with her.

Althea	Oh, no!
Jane	What's wrong?
Althea	It's a letter from the bank. My check bounced, and I have to pay $15.
Jane	How did that happen?
Althea	I wrote a check for $48.99 to pay for a dress, but I only had $39.24 in my checking account.
Jane	Didn't you deposit your paycheck?
Althea	No, I forgot to. I have to be more careful next time.

■ Comprehension Questions

1. Why did Althea's check bounce?

_____

2. Why didn't Althea deposit her paycheck?

_____

3. How much did the bank charge Althea? Why is there a charge?

_____

 **Reading**

When Althea opened her checking account, the bank gave her an ATM (automated teller machine) card. This machine is called an automated teller because it takes the place of the teller inside the bank.

Althea can go to the machine, put her ATM card in, and enter her secret number. Now she is ready to do her banking. The machine will automatically credit her deposits and deduct her withdrawals from her checking account. Althea must remember to add the deposits or subtract the withdrawals from the balance in her check book. The ATM prints a receipt for Althea each time she uses the machine.

Using the ATM is very convenient for Althea because she does not have to go into the bank every time she wants to deposit or withdraw money.

Also, Althea can use the ATM at any branch of her bank. Althea does not have to be near her bank branch to makes deposits or withdrawals.

Here is what Althea's ATM card looks like:

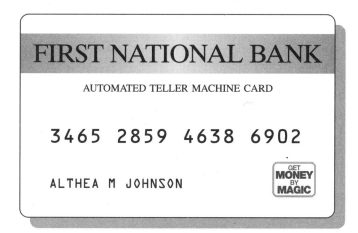

FIRST NATIONAL BANK

AUTOMATED TELLER MACHINE CARD

3465 2859 4638 6902

ALTHEA M JOHNSON

GET MONEY BY MAGIC

■ **Comprehension Questions**

Write the answers to the following questions.

1. How can Althea make a deposit or withdrawal without going into the bank?

_____

2. How does Althea keep a record of her deposits and withdrawals when she uses the ATM?

_____

3. Why is having an ATM convenient?

_____

 **Reading**

Applying for a Credit Card

Althea went to the bank three weeks ago. She deposited money in her checking account. She decided to apply for a credit card. Althea can use it in almost all stores, restaurants, hotels, gas stations, etc. She can use it instead of cash. Althea filled out an application.

Here is an example of a credit card application:

MasterCard Credit Card Application

Applicant Information (Please print)

Last name	First name	Middle name	Birthday	Telephone number ( )
Present street address		Apt. no.	At present address _____ Yrs. _____ Mos.	☐ Rent ☐ Buying ☐ Live with Parents
City	State	ZIP Code	Social security no.	Education ☐ Grade school ☐ High school
Previous address		Apt. no.	At previous address _____ Yrs. _____ Mos.	☐ Part college ☐ College degree ☐ Graduate degree
City	State	ZIP code	Driver's license no.	Dependents No. _____ Ages _____
Name and address of nearest relative not living with you			Relationship	Telephone number ( )
Present employer			Position (If self-employed, give nature of business) _____ Yrs. _____ Mos.	
Street address			Business telephone ( )	Monthly job income
City	State	ZIP code	Previous employer	
Previous employer address			Position _____ Yrs. _____ Mos.	
Source of other income, if any (Alimony, child support, or separate maintenance income need not be revealed if you do not wish to have it considered as a basis for repaying this obligation.)				Monthly Amount

Asset and Debt Information

Autos owned (state whose name registered)		License no.	Make/model/year	Value
Cash value of life insurance			Issuer	Face value
Real estate and location			Date acquired	Value
Bank with checking account		Branch	Acct. no.	Balance
Bank with savings account		Branch	Acct. no.	Balance

List banks, department stores, finance companies (including alimony/child support obligations)

Name of creditor	Branch or location	Account number	Balance	Monthly payment

Last week Althea received her credit card. Yesterday she used it for the first time. She bought a new answering machine for $59.84. She paid for it with her credit card. This is how: She gave her credit card to the clerk. The clerk rang up the purchase on the register, and the register printed a charge slip. Althea signed the slip and gave it back to the clerk. Then the register printed another copy for her. Althea should keep her copy because it's a record of her purchase.

Here is the charge slip:

```
            THE OFFICE STORE
          PITTSBURGH, PA 15257

0222 00003 04682              03/16/96
SALE 471                      03:11 PM

045672947625 ANS MACHINE          56.99
              SUBTOTAL             56.99
              TAX 5%                2.85
              TOTAL               59.84
62623123123110 VISA/MC           59.84
AUTH CODE 012367/2062846             TA


ORIGINAL RECEIPT REQUIRED FOR REFUND


     THANK YOU FOR SHOPPING AT
          THE OFFICE STORE
```

Once a month Althea receives a bill in the mail from the credit card company. It lists the stores where she used her credit card and the amounts she charged during that month.

Here is the bill she received for the answering machine:

Important: Please retain this portion of your statement. It is your permanent record.

Account 626 23123 123 110
Credit Limit $1,000.00
Available Credit $940.16

Statement Date 03/18/96
Payment Due Date 04/10/96
Minimum Payment Due $10.00

ACCOUNT SUMMARY

Previous Balance	Payments Credits	Purchases	Cash Advances	Finance Charges	New Balance
0.00	-0.00	59.84	0.00	0.00	59.84

TO AVOID ADDITIONAL FINANCE CHARGES AND FEES, PAY THE NEW BALANCE IN FULL BY THE DUE DATE.

FINANCE CHARGES

Annual Percentage Rate	Daily Periodic Rate
18.00%	0.04931%

TRANSACTIONS

Trans Date	Post Date	Reference Number	Description	Amount
03/16	03/16	34869502F3547GP0R0	The Office Store, Pittsburgh, PA	59.84

She should pay the bill within 25 days of the billing date. If she doesn't pay the bill in 25 days, she must pay 1½% interest each month or 18% interest a year.

Althea uses her credit card because it's convenient. With her credit card she can buy things now and pay for them later. But Althea must be careful. Some people use credit cards too much. At the end of the month, they receive their bills and they don't have enough money to pay them. Then they must pay a high interest. Althea must remember to buy only what she needs and what she can afford.

■ **Comprehension Questions**

Write the answers to the following questions.

1. Why did Althea go to the bank three weeks ago?

   _____

2. What is a credit card?

   _____

3. Where can Althea use it?

   _____

4. What information did Althea have to fill out on the application?

   _____

5. How long did it take for Althea to receive her credit card?

   _____

6. What did Althea buy with her credit card? How much was it?

   _____

7. What information is on the charge form?

   _____

8. Why should Althea keep her copy of the charge form?

   _____

9. How often does Althea receive her credit card bill?

   _____

10. What information is on the bill?

_____

11. Why should Althea pay the bill within 25 days of the billing date?

_____

12. Why does Althea use her credit card?

_____

13. Why does Althea have to be careful when she buys on credit?

_____

 # Listening Comprehension

A. Circle the number that your teacher says.

1. Althea's address is   1727   7027   Walnut Street.

2. Mr. Franco completed the application for a new job in   13   30   minutes.

3. Quan paid $15.37 $50.37   for a new pair of shoes.

4. Althea was   14   40   minutes late for class last night.

5. Mr. Wilson bought three books last week. They cost $16.95. $60.95.

6. Charlie spent   19   90   minutes fixing a car.

7. Charlie has $18 $80   in his pocket.

8. Mayling withdrew $13.50 $30.50   from her savings account.

9. Quan and Mayling live at   1463   4063   Highland Avenue.

10. Tomatoes cost $1.19 $.75   a pound today in the supermarket.

B. Fill in the blanks with the number that your teacher says. Remember to use the dollar sign and the decimal point.

Althea has to pay the following bills this month Her electric bill is _____. Her

gas bill is _____. Her water bill is _____. Her telephone bill this month is _____. Althea went to the doctor. She pays him _____ a

month. Althea's rent is _____ a month. She bought a new answering machine.

She used her credit card. The answering machine cost _____.

 # Problem Solving

Checking

A. Yesterday, Althea paid her bills. Look at the check she wrote for her electric bill. She must write checks with a *pen,* not a pencil.

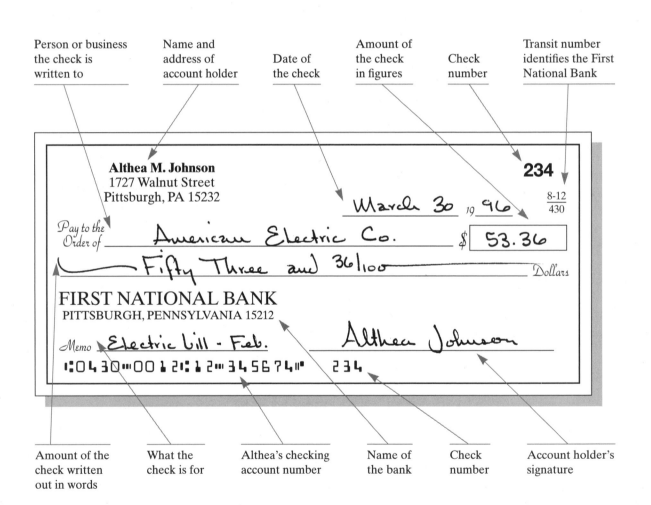

Person or business the check is written to

Name and address of account holder

Date of the check

Amount of the check in figures

Check number

Transit number identifies the First National Bank

Althea M. Johnson
1727 Walnut Street
Pittsburgh, PA 15232

234

8-12 / 430

Pay to the Order of ___ *American Electric Co.* ___ $ 53.36

Fifty Three and 36/100 _____ Dollars

FIRST NATIONAL BANK
PITTSBURGH, PENNSYLVANIA 15212

Memo *Electric bill - Feb.*

Althea Johnson

⑆0430⑈0012⑆12⑈3456741⑈ 234

Amount of the check written out in words

What the check is for

Althea's checking account number

Name of the bank

Check number

Account holder's signature

Write a check for Althea to pay her gas bill:

Columbia Gas Co. $13.21

Althea M. Johnson   **235**
1727 Walnut Street
Pittsburgh, PA 15232

_____ 19_____   8-12/430

Pay to the
Order of _____ $ _____

_____ Dollars

FIRST NATIONAL BANK
PITTSBURGH, PENNSYLVANIA 15212

Memo _____

⑆0430⑈0012⑆12⑈3456740⑈ 235

Now, write out each amount that Althea must pay for her bills.

1. Check #234: American Electric Co. $53.36

   _____

2. Check #235: Columbia Gas Co. $13.21

   _____

3. Check #236: City Water Co. $24

   _____

4. Check #237: People's Telephone Co. $41

   _____

5. Check #238: Dr. Lee Morrison $65

   _____

6. Check #239: Acme Realty Co. $500

   _____

7. Check #240: MasterCard $59.84

_____

B. Balance Althea's checkbook. Enter each check and then deduct the amount from the balance. What is her balance after she pays her bills?

Be sure to **deduct** any fees which may affect your balance, such as monthly maintenance charges and automated teller machine fees.

Item Number	Date	Description	Subtractions Amt. of Payment		✓ T	(−) Fee	Additions Amt. of Payment		BALANCE 132 41	
	3/16	Deposit					762	50	762	50
									894	91
234	3/30	American Electric Co.	53	36					53	36
									841	55

Remember to record automatic payments and deposits on date authorized.

C. At the end of the month, Althea's going to receive a bank statement in the mail from First National Bank. Her bank statement tells her how much money she has in her account. Check her bank statement with her checkbook. Did the bank pay all her checks? Althea's canceled checks are her receipts. What should she do with them? According to the bank, Althea has $138.35 in her account. If she writes a check for $142, the check will *bounce*. The bank charges her a service charge if one of her checks bounces.

FIRST NATIONAL BANK
of Pittsburgh, PA

Ms. Althea M. Johnson
1727 Walnut Street
Pittsburgh, PA 15232

Date of Statement	04/30/96	Beginning Balance	132.41
Account Number	12345674	Deposits This Period	762.50
No. Deposits This Period	1	Debits This Period	756.56
No. Debits This Period	7	Closing Balance	138.35

Date	Checks and Debits		Deposits and Credits	Balance
				132.41
3/16			762.50	894.91
3/30	234	53.36		841.55
3/30	235	13.36		828.19
3/30	236	24.00		804.19
3/30	237	41.00		763.19
3/30	238	65.00		698.19
3/30	239	500.00		198.19
4/01	240	59.84		138.35

D. Althea deposited her paycheck in her checking account on March 16. She endorsed it at the bank. She did not endorse it before she arrived. This is how she endorsed it.

PAYROLL CHECK	*Sunshine Travel*		225012
	435 E. 6TH STREET	5-9 / 420	
	PITTSBURGH, PA 15112		

PAY   Seven hundred sixty two and 50/100 dollars

DATE   03/13/96

TO THE ORDER OF   Althea M. Johnson
1727 Walnut Street
Pittsburgh, PA 15232

AMOUNT $762.50

Fidelity Bank
Pittsburgh, PA

James C. Roberts
Charles R. South

⑆225012⑈ ⑇0143⑈0079⑈ 633⑈56⑈

ENDORSE HERE

Althea M. Johnson
FOR DEPOSIT ONLY

DO NOT WRITE BELOW THIS LINE

She must endorse the check exactly the way it's paid to her. If Althea wants to cash her check, she doesn't write "For Deposit Only." She writes only her name.

Althea filled out a deposit slip to deposit her check. Here is a sample of the deposit slip. Fill it out for Althea.

CHECKING ACCOUNT DEPOSIT TICKET

Althea M. Johnson
1727 Walnut Street
Pittsburgh, PA 15232

Date _____ 19_____

_____
SIGN HERE FOR CASH RECEIVED

First National Bank
Pittsburgh, PA 15212

⑇0430⑈0012⑈ 12⑈345674⑈

CURRENCY		
COIN		
CHECKS LIST SINGLY		
TOTAL		
LESS CASH RECEIVED		
NET DEPOSIT		

Supermarkets

 Learner Objectives

Consumer Competencies

- Being able to prepare a shopping list and to list the items according to the departments in a supermarket
- Developing an understanding of some of the basic rules to follow when shopping in a supermarket
- Being able to recognize and use the names and abbreviations of containers, units, and measures
- Understanding how items are grouped in a supermarket and where to find them. Becoming familiar with the information on a food label
- Being able to understand the basic ideas of unit pricing and to do some computation on unit pricing

Grammatical Structures

- Being able to understand and use the following structures: countable/noncountable nouns with *some/any, much/many, a little/a few/a lot of*; prepositions of location; and indirect questions

Vocabulary Items

- Being able to understand and use the following words in context:

Nouns		Verbs	Adjectives
abbreviation	item	advertise	crowded
aisle	label	check out	on sale
baking needs	measure	put away	
bargain	net weight		
brand	nutritional		
container	information		
dairy products	produce		
department	product		
express lane	shelf		
fight	specials		
frozen food	unit		
grocery	unit price		
household cleaners	volume		
ingredient			

 # Dialogue

Quan went to the supermarket. He is home now. He and Mayling are putting away the groceries. They are having an argument.

Mayling	Quan, why did you buy steak? How much was it?
Quan	$3.70 a pound.
Mayling	$3.70 a pound! I wrote two pounds of hamburger on the list. Why didn't you buy hamburger?
Quan	Because I like steak.
Mayling	Quan, we made a budget. We can't buy steak every week on our budget. It's expensive. We spend too much money on food.
Quan	I know, but I'm tired of hamburger!
Mayling	A small bottle of laundry detergent! The small bottle is expensive. I wrote a large bottle of laundry detergent on the list.
Quan	What list?
Mayling	The shopping list. I gave it to you before you went to the supermarket.
Quan	I don't like to use a list. I buy what we need and what I want.
Mayling	When we use a list, we buy only what we need. We save money that way.
Quan	Lists aren't important. They're not necessary.
Mayling	Well, I think they are. Let's ask Mr. Wilson, our Consumer Education teacher, about this.

■ **Comprehension Questions**

1. Where did Quan go?

_____

2. What are he and Mayling doing now?

_____

3. What did Quan buy? How much did it cost?

_____

4. What did Mayling write on the list?

_____

5. Why did Quan buy steak? Why should he buy hamburger instead of steak?

_____

6. What size bottle of laundry detergent did Quan buy?

_____

7. Did Quan use the list? Why not? How does Quan shop?

_____

8. Why does Mayling think they should use a list?

_____

9. What are they going to ask Mr. Wilson?

_____

 # Grammar

Some/Any

We use the words *some* and *any* to indicate an indefinite quantity. We use both *some* and *any* in questions although *any* is more common. We use *some* in affirmative statements and *any* in negative statements.

Question Form	Do we have any potatoes?
	Do we have some potatoes?
Affirmative	Yes, we have some potatoes.
Negative	No, we don't have any potatoes.
Short Answer	Yes, we have some.
	Yes, we do.
	No, we don't have any.
	No, we don't.

■ Exercises

A. Quan went to he supermarket this morning. Mayling wants to make lunch now, but she needs to know what Quan bought. To find out what Quan bought, form questions and answers using the following items with *some* or *any*.

Example: Bread

      Mayling Did you buy any bread?

          Quan Yes, <u>I bought some bread</u>
                   or
              Yes, <u>I bought some.</u>
                   or
              Yes, <u>I did.</u>

1. Milk

   Mayling _____

      Quan Yes, _____

2. Soup

   Mayling _____

      Quan No, _____

3. Crackers

   Mayling _____

      Quan No, _____

4. Peanut butter

   Mayling _____

      Quan Yes, _____

5. Jelly

   Mayling _____

      Quan Yes, _____

6. Ham

   Mayling _____

      Quan Yes, _____

7. Mustard

   Mayling _____

      Quan No, _____

8. Cheese

Mayling _____

    Quan No, _____

9. Coke

Mayling _____

    Quan Yes, _____

10. Potato chips

Mayling _____

    Quan No, _____

B. Make sentences with *didn't have any* and *needed some* for these situations.

Example: Mayling ate the last piece of bread. Quan wanted to make a sandwich.

    Quan didn't have any bread.

    He needed some bread.

1. Quan used the last egg for breakfast. Mayling wanted to bake a cake.

_____

_____

2. Nilda and Charlie wanted to drive to the mountains, but the gas tank was empty.

_____

_____

3. Mr. and Mrs. Franco ate an excellent dinner at a restaurant. Mr. Franco wanted to pay the bill, but his wallet was empty.

_____

_____

4. Mayling used all the shampoo. Quan wanted to wash his hair.

_____

_____

 **Reading**

In their Consumer Education class, Mayling and Quan read the following information about supermarket shopping.

Before you go to the supermarket, you should check to see what you have at home. Look in your refrigerator and freezer. Also, be sure to check your kitchen cabinets to see if you have sugar, salt, bread, etc. Then, you should make a list of what you need. Organize the list according to the departments in the supermarket. For example, list all the dairy products—milk, eggs, butter, etc.—together.

At the supermarket, you should buy only what you need and what you can use. Supermarkets advertise a lot and offer "specials" because they want you to buy a lot. Be careful. And remember these important points. Don't shop when you're hungry, tired, or in a hurry, and don't shop when the stores are crowded.

■ Comprehension Questions

Write the answers to the following questions.

1. What should you do before you go to the supermarket?

   _____

2. How should you organize your shopping list?

   _____

3. Should you buy all the specials at the supermarket? Why or why not?

   _____

4. When shouldn't you go to the supermarket? Why?

   _____

5. Why should you be careful when you shop at a supermarket?

   _____

6. Should you be careful when you shop at other stores? Why?

   _____

Grammar

Countable/Noncountable Nouns

Countable Nouns

We can count some nouns, for example, apples, bananas, children. These are countable nouns. Countable nouns can take an indefinite article in the singular, and they have plural forms.

We can say: a banana   a child
               one banana   one child
               ten bananas   ten children
               some bananas   some children

Noncountable Nouns

We cannot count some nouns in their original mass form, for example, *milk, water, oil.* These are noncountable nouns. Noncountable nouns cannot take an indefinite article and do not have a plural form. We do not use *a, one, two,* etc. before them. We use the singular form of the verb with them.

We say: milk
             some milk

Some nouns may be countable or noncountable, depending on their meaning. For example:

The *food* was delicious. (noncountable)
Convenience *foods* are popular with busy people. (countable)

■ Exercises

A. Here is a list of the names of the items in the pictures on the next page. Write the name of each item under the picture. Are these items countable or noncountable?

sugar	rice	margarine
cereal	carrots	milk
chicken	cheese	salad dressing
broom	pineapple	laundry detergent
mop	bread	salt
lettuce	bananas	soup
coffee	eggs	

B. To count noncountable nouns, we put a unit of measure and *of* before them. For example:

> a *bottle* of milk
> three *slices* of cheese
> five *pounds* of flour

We can also use these names of containers (a bottle), units (three slices), and measures (five pounds) with countable nouns. Here is a list of containers, units, and measures.

Containers

bag (of potatoes, apples, sugar, flour, candy, potato chips)

bottle (of ketchup, oil, soda, laundry detergent)

box (of laundry detergent, cereal, crackers, salt, rice)

can (of soup, soda, coffee, vegetables, tuna, tomato sauce)

carton (of eggs)

jar (of mustard, peanut butter, mayonnaise, olives, pickles)

pack (of gum)

package (of cheese, napkins, hot dogs)

Units

bar (of soap)

bunch (of bananas, grapes, carrots, celery)

cup (of flour, sugar)

dozen/half a dozen (donuts, eggs, cookies)
  Note: We do not use *of* after *dozen*.

head (of lettuce)

loaf (of bread); *plural* – loaves of bread

piece (of cake, candy, bubble gum, fish)

slice (of cheese, bacon, bread, meat, ham)

Measures

U.S. System		Metric System	
Liquid	**Dry**	**Liquid**	**Dry**
8 fl. oz. = 1 cup	16 oz. = 1 lb.	1 fl. oz. = .03 liter	1 oz. = 28 grams
2 cups = 1 pt.	8 oz. = 1 cup	1 qt. = .95 liter	3.5 oz. = 100 grams
16 oz. = 1 pt.		1 gal. = 3.79 liters	1 lb. = .45 kilograms
4 cups = 1 qt.		33.8 fl. oz. = 1 liter	2.2 lbs. = 1 kilogram
2 pt. = 1 qt.			
32 oz. = 1 qt.			
4 qt. = 1 gal.			
128 oz. = 1 gal.			

Abbreviations*

ounce = oz.	quart = qt.
fluid ounce = fl. oz.	gallon = gal.
pound = lb.	dozen = doz.
pint = pt.	

*Abbreviations are the same in the singular and plural.

Look at the pictures on page 74 again. Write names of containers, units, and measures that we can use with each item.

 **Grammar**

Much/Many

We use the word *much* with noncountable nouns and *many* with countable nouns. To ask about quantity we say *How much* or *How many*. For example:

How many apples do you need?
How much cheese do you need?

■ Exercises

A. Look at the pictures on page 74 again. Decide if each of the items is countable or noncountable. Write the word *many* next to the countable items and *much* next to the noncountable items.

B. Charlie and Nilda are planning a dinner party for eight people. They are making a shopping list. Fill in the blanks with *How much* or *How many*.

Example: **Charlie** <u>How much</u> rice should we buy?
         Nilda One box.

1. **Charlie** _____ meat should we buy?
    Nilda Four pounds.

2. **Charlie** _____ lettuce should we buy?
    Nilda Two heads.

3. **Charlie** _____ tomatoes should we buy?
    Nilda Two pounds.

4. **Charlie** _____ cucumbers should we buy?
    Nilda Three.

5. **Charlie** _____ soda should we buy?
    Nilda Four bottles.

Continue this conversation between Nilda and Charlie. Make questions with *How much* or *How many*. Answer the questions with the name of a container, a unit, or a measure.

6. onions _____

_____

7. coffee _____

_____

8. milk _____

_____

9. butter _____

_____

10. carrots _____

_____

11. bread _____

_____

12. salad dressing _____

_____

13. fruit _____

_____

14. napkins _____

_____

15. ice cream _____

_____

 # Grammar

A Little/A Few/A Lot Of

We use the words *a little* with noncountable nouns and *a few* with countable nouns to indicate a small quantity. *A lot* indicates a large quantity. We use *a lot of* with both countable and noncountable nouns.

Countable Nouns

Question Form	Do you want a lot of apples?
Affirmative	I want a lot of apples. I want a few apples.
Negative	I don't want a lot of apples.
Short Answer	Yes, I want a lot. *or* Yes, I do. No, I want a few. *or* No, I don't.

Noncountable Nouns

Question Form	Do you want a lot of rice?
Affirmative	I want a lot of rice. I want a little rice.
Negative	I don't want a lot of rice.
Short Answer	Yes, I want a lot. *or* Yes, I do. No, I want a little. *or* No, I don't.

■ Exercises

A. Look at the pictures on page 74 again. Write *a little* next to noncountable items and *a few* next to countable items.

B. Write the opposite. Use *a little* or *a few.*

Example: I want a lot of bread.

    <u>I want a little bread.</u>

1. I cooked a lot of bacon.

    _____

2. I drank a lot of milk.

    _____

3. I need a lot of money.

    _____

4. I chewed a lot of gum.

_____

5. I ate a lot of ice cream.

_____

6. I ate a lot of peanuts.

_____

7. I bought a lot of fruit.

_____

8. I ate a lot of sandwiches.

_____

9. I want a lot of potato chips.

_____

10. I drank a lot of orange juice.

_____

C. Make questions in the past tense with the item, the verb, and _a lot of._ Answer the questions with _only a few_ or _only a little._

Example: buy/spinach

<u>Did you buy a lot of spinach?</u>

<u>No, only a little.</u>

1. buy/toothpaste

_____

_____

2. drink/coffee

_____

_____

3. eat/bread

_____

_____

4. eat/chicken

_____

_____

5. cook/fish

_____

_____

6. buy/cereal

_____

_____

7. eat/strawberries

_____

_____

8 drink/milk

_____

_____

9. buy/lemons

_____

_____

10. cook/potatoes

_____

_____

D. Make questions with *How much* or *How many.* Answer with *Only a few* or *Only a little.*

Example: Althea doesn't like eggs. She eats only three eggs a month.

How many eggs does Althea eat?

Only a few.

1. Quan bought 50 ounces of laundry detergent at the supermarket last week. Mayling usually buys 100 ounces.

   _____

   _____

2. Charlie's home only about two evenings a week. The other evenings he's with Nilda.

   _____

   _____

3. Mr. Franco loves cake, but he eats only two pieces of cake a week.

   _____

   _____

4. Yesterday, Mayling drank a half a glass of orange juice.

   _____

   _____

5. Charlie and Nilda went shopping downtown only two or three times last month.

   _____

   _____

6. Mr. Wilson doesn't like fish very much. He eats fish only about once a week.

   _____

   _____

7. Mr. and Mrs. Franco used only two or three pounds of coffee last year.

   _____

   _____

8. Mrs. Franco spends $90 a week on groceries.

_____

_____

9. Last week Charlie had dinner at home only three times.

_____

_____

10. Mr. Franco drinks coffee only in the morning, and then he drinks only one cup.

_____

_____

E. Althea's checking to see what she needs at the supermarket. Her friend Jane is helping her. Jane's making a list of the items that Althea needs.

Jane Do you have any milk?

Althea _Only a little._ _____

Jane _How much_ _____ milk do you need?

Althea I need _one carton._ _____

Follow the pattern. Answer the first question with _Only a little_ or _Only a few._ Answer the questions _How much_ or _How many_ with the name of a container, a unit, or a measure.

1. **Jane** Do you have any rice?

Althea _____

Jane _____ rice do you need.

Althea I need _____

2. **Jane** Do you have any peanut butter?

Althea _____

Jane _____ peanut butter do you need?

Althea I need _____

3.   **Jane**   Do you have any cheese?

     Althea _____

     Jane _____ cheese do you need?

     Althea   I need _____

4.   **Jane**   Do you have any soup?

     Althea _____

     Jane _____ soup do you need?

     Althea   I need _____

5.   **Jane**   Do you have any coffee?

     Althea _____

     Jane _____ coffee do you need?

     Althea   I need _____

6.   **Jane**   Do you have any cereal?

     Althea _____

     Jane _____ cereal do you need?

     Althea   I need _____

7.   **Jane**   Do you have any bread?

     Althea _____

     Jane _____ bread do you need?

     Althea   I need _____

8.   **Jane**   Do you have any orange juice?

     Althea _____

     Jane _____ orange juice do you need?

     Althea   I need _____

? Problem Solving

Althea needs to buy the following items at the supermarket.

milk	bananas	bread	fresh mushrooms
rice	cheese	hamburger	laundry detergent
soup	coffee	cereal	frozen orange juice
sugar	napkins	peanut butter	tomato sauce

Make a shopping list for Althea. Here are the departments in the supermarket. Write each item under the department where Althea can find it.

Dairy Products   **Baking Needs**

Produce   **Cereal**

Canned Vegetables   **Household Cleaners**
(including soup, tuna, tomato sauce)

Bread   **Paper Products**

Frozen Foods   **Other Grocery Items**
                                      (including salad dressing, mustard,
                                      peanut butter, coffee, tea, rice, pasta)

Meat

Grammar

Prepositions of Location: *in, on, next to, between*

Imagine that you work in a supermarket. The customers ask you many questions about where different items are. Answer the questions according to the diagram on the next page of Aisle 4 in the supermarket. Use this pattern:

Customer Excuse me, can you tell me where the cake mixes are?

 You Yes, they're in Aisle 4, on the bottom shelf, between the baking soda and the oil.

AISLE 4

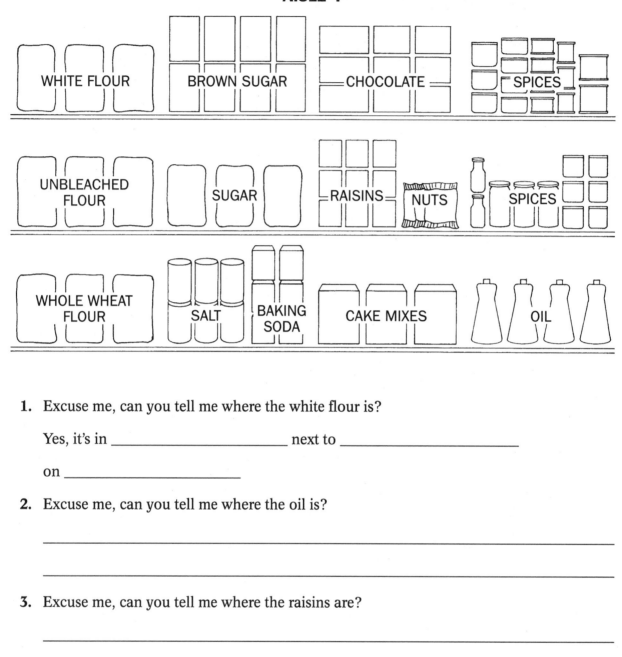

1. Excuse me, can you tell me where the white flour is?

   Yes, it's in _____ next to _____

   on _____

2. Excuse me, can you tell me where the oil is?

   _____

   _____

3. Excuse me, can you tell me where the raisins are?

   _____

   _____

4. Excuse me, can you tell me where the spices are?

   _____

   _____

5. Excuse me, can you tell me where the sugar is?

_____

_____

6. Excuse me, can you tell me where the chocolate is?

_____

_____

7. Excuse me, can you tell me where the salt is?

_____

_____

8. Excuse me, can you tell me where the whole wheat flour is?

_____

_____

9. Excuse me, can you tell me where the baking soda is?

_____

_____

10. Excuse me, can you tell me where the nuts are?

_____

_____

 # Dialogue

Mayling went shopping today. She and Quan are putting away the groceries.

> **Quan** Look at all these tomatoes! How many pounds did you buy?
>
> **Mayling** Six
>
> **Quan** Six! Mayling, you know I don't like tomatoes. I never eat them. Why did you buy so many?

Mayling Because they were on sale, three pounds for three dollars.

Quan What are we going to do with all these tomatoes?

Mayling I don't know. But, look, I bought chicken. It was on sale $.79 a pound.

Quan That's good. We can have chicken for dinner this week. Mayling, I think we should buy only the specials when we're going to use the food.

Mayling I know. You're right, Quan. But I can't pass up a bargain!

■ Comprehension Questions

1. Why did Mayling buy so many tomatoes?

   _____

2. Why shouldn't she buy a lot of tomatoes?

   _____

3. Why did Mayling buy chicken?

   _____

4. When should you buy the specials?

   _____

 # Grammar

Indirect Questions

In the supermarket, to find out where something is, we ask:

Excuse me, where is the peanut butter?

However, sometimes we want to be more polite, so we use the introductory phrases *Can you tell me* and *Do you know* before the questions. We say:

Excuse me, can you tell me where the peanut butter is?
Excuse me, do you know where the peanut butter is?

Sometimes, in small grocery stores, there are no prices on the items. We would say:

Excuse me, how much does this jar of peanut butter cost?
Excuse me, can you tell me how much this jar of peanut butter costs?

■ Exercises

A. You are at a new supermarket. You need to know where some of the items on your shopping list are. Form polite questions with *Can you tell me* and *Do you know* to ask the location of the items. Answer the questions according to the map on the next page.

Example: 1 dozen oranges

> Excuse me, can you tell me where the oranges are?
> Yes, they're in the produce department.

Shopping List

5 lb. of sugar

2 cans of peaches

1 can of tuna

2 bottles of 7-Up

1 bag of oatmeal cookies

1 can of coffee

10 lb. of laundry detergent

1/2 gallon of ice cream

1 lb. of frozen fish

1 lb. of onions

2 loaves of bread

1 lb. of margarine

1 package of hot dogs

1 container of cottage cheese

1 lb. of fresh mushrooms

1 doz. eggs

3 containers of yogurt

3 cans of frozen orange juice

5 lb. of chuck roast

1 jar of peanut butter

MEAT   pork, beef, chicken, seafood, hot dogs, sausage, bacon, lunch meats

BREAD   cakes, rolls

DAIRY PRODUCTS   milk, eggs, cheese, butter, yogurt

PRODUCE   fresh fruit, fresh vegetables

1 Canned fruit, canned juice

2 Canned vegetables, soup, tuna, tomato sauce

3 Salad dressing, ketchup, mustard, peanut butter, jelly, coffee, tea, rice, pasta

4 Baking needs, flour, sugar, salt, spices, oil, cake mixes

5 Cereal, crackers, cookies

6 Beverages, potato chips, candy

7 Paper products, napkins, paper towels

8 Household cleaners, household needs, detergent, soap, shampoo, toothpaste, aspirin

9 Frozen food, juice, ice cream, TV dinners, pie, cake, vegetables, French fries, fish

CHECK OUT

EXPRESS LANE

10 items or less
Cash only

CHECK CASHING

SHOPPING CARTS

ENTRANCE

B. There is no price on some of the items that you want to buy. You want to know the price. Form polite question with *Can you tell me* and *Do you know* to ask the price of the following items. Use *this* and *these.* Answer the questions.

Example: Rice   ($1.19/box)

Excuse me, can you tell me how much this rice is?

Yes, it's $1.19 a box.

1. Potato chips   (99¢/bag)

2. Milk   ($1.57/½ gallon)

3. Lettuce   (99¢/head)

4. Cereal   ($2.49/box)

5. Peanut butter   ($1.69/jar)

6. Yogurt   (60¢/container)

7. Hamburger   ($1.99/lb.)

8. Sliced ham   ($1.95/package)

_____

_____

9. Frozen cauliflower   (59¢/box)

_____

_____

10. Mustard   (89¢/jar)

_____

_____

 # Reading

Labels

You should learn to read and understand labels. A label has a lot of information that you need to determine the best quality and the best price. Look at this food label. It has the following information.

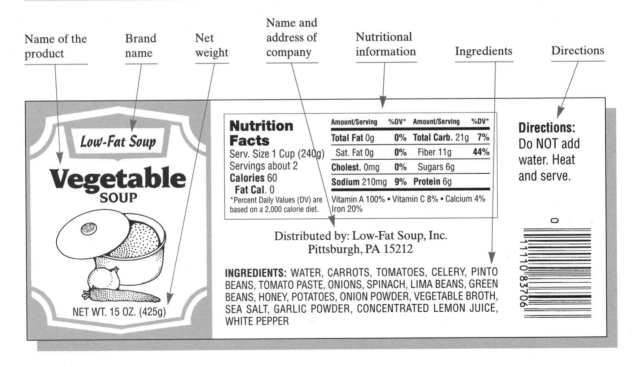

Name of the product   Brand name   Net weight   Name and address of company   Nutritional information   Ingredients   Directions

Low-Fat Soup

Vegetable SOUP

NET WT. 15 OZ. (425g)

Nutrition Facts
Serv. Size 1 Cup (240g)
Servings about 2
Calories 60
 Fat Cal. 0
*Percent Daily Values (DV) are based on a 2,000 calorie diet.

Amount/Serving	%DV*	Amount/Serving	%DV*
Total Fat 0g	**0%**	**Total Carb.** 21g	**7%**
Sat. Fat 0g	**0%**	Fiber 11g	**44%**
Cholest. 0mg	**0%**	Sugars 6g	
Sodium 210mg	**9%**	**Protein** 6g	

Vitamin A 100% • Vitamin C 8% • Calcium 4% • Iron 20%

Distributed by: Low-Fat Soup, Inc.
Pittsburgh, PA 15212

INGREDIENTS: WATER, CARROTS, TOMATOES, CELERY, PINTO BEANS, TOMATO PASTE, ONIONS, SPINACH, LIMA BEANS, GREEN BEANS, HONEY, POTATOES, ONION POWDER, VEGETABLE BROTH, SEA SALT, GARLIC POWDER, CONCENTRATED LEMON JUICE, WHITE PEPPER

Directions: Do NOT add water. Heat and serve.

Name of the Product, Brand Name, and Company Name and Address

The name of the product, the brand name, and the name and address of the company that made the product must be on the label.

Net Weight (net wt.)

The net weight must be on the label. It tells you the weight of the food without the container.

Directions

The directions tell you the best way to prepare the product.

Ingredients

The label tells you the items that the product contains. These items are the ingredients. The ingredients are in order of quantity. The main ingredient is first. The label of this product tells you that the soup contains more water than any other ingredient.

Nutritional Information

The label tells you the number of servings in the container, the number of calories per serving, and the amount of protein, carbohydrates, and fat per serving. The label also tells you the percentage of a person's daily food need that the product supplies.

Date

In many states, milk must have a date on it. The date tells you the last day the product should be sold. The label says "sell by" or "not to be sold after" and the date. Sometimes, other items such as dairy products, bread, and meat also have dates on them.

■ Comprehension Questions

Write the answers to the following questions.

1. Why should you learn to read and understand labels?

   _____

2. What information is on a label?

   _____

3. What is the net weight?

   _____

4. In what order does the label list the ingredients?

   _____

5. What nutritional information does the label contain?

   _____

6. What does the date on milk tell you?

 # Reading

Unit Pricing

When you are shopping in the supermarket, you should compare prices. To determine the best price, first compare the net weights. If the net weights of the two items are the same, compare the prices to determine the cheapest.

If the net weights are not the same, you have to find out the unit price. The unit price is the price of an item per unit measure, for example, one ounce, one quart, one pound. Supermarkets give you this information. They tell you the name of the item, weight, unit price, and the price that you pay. If the supermarket doesn't have unit pricing, you can determine it. To determine the unit price, divide the price of the item by the net weight, or volume. For example:

The 16-fl.-oz. (1 pt.) bottle of vegetable oil costs 95¢. The 38-fl.-oz. (1 qt. oz.) bottle costs $2.09, and the 48-fl.-oz. (1 qt. 1 pt.) bottle costs $2.45. To compare the prices, you need to know the price per ounce of each bottle. Divide the price by the weight in ounces:

$ .95 \div 16$ fl. oz. $= .059$/ounce
$2.09 \div 38$ fl. oz. $= .055$/ounce
$2.45 \div 48$ fl. oz. $= .051$/ounce

Therefore, the largest size, 48 fl. oz., is the best buy because the price per ounce is the cheapest.

■ Comprehension Questions

Write the answers to the following questions.

1. What does unit price mean?

2. How can you determine the unit price of an item?

Listening Comprehension

A. Listen to the following conversations. Fill in the blanks based on the information in the conversation.

Example: *Your teacher says:*
Excuse me, can you tell me where the sugar is?
Yes, it's in Aisle 4, on the middle shelf, next to the flour.

You write:

Item: <u>sugar</u>   Aisle: <u>4</u>

Shelf: <u>middle</u>   Next to: <u>flour</u>

1. Item: _____   Aisle: _____

   Shelf: _____   Next to: _____

2. Item: _____   Aisle: _____

   Shelf: _____   Next to: _____

3. Item: _____   Aisle: _____

   Shelf: _____   Next to: _____

4. Item: _____   Aisle: _____

   Shelf: _____   Next to: _____

5. Item: _____   Aisle: _____

   Shelf: _____   Next to: _____

6. Item: _____   Aisle: _____

   Shelf: _____   Next to: _____

7. Item: _____   Aisle: _____

   Shelf: _____   Next to: _____

8. Item: _____   Department: _____

   Next to: _____

9. Item: _____   Department: _____

Next to: _____

10. Item: _____   Aisle: _____

Shelf: _____   Next to: _____

B. Listen to the following conversations. Fill in the blanks based on the information in the conversation.

Example: *Your teacher says:*
Excuse me, do you know how much this bag of sugar costs?
Yes, it's $1.89.

You write:

Item: _sugar_____

Price: _$1.89_____ / _bag_____

1. Item: _____

Price: _____ / _____

2. Item: _____

Price: _____ / _____

3. Item: _____

Price: _____ / _____

4. Item: _____

Price: _____ / _____

5. Item: _____

Price: _____ / _____

Problem Solving

Unit Pricing

Compare the prices of the following products. Determine the unit price. Which brand or size is the best buy?

Name of Product	Net Weight	Price	Unit Price	Best Buy
1. Clean-O Laundry Detergent	50 oz.	$2.99		☐
	100 oz.	$4.99		☐
2. Wendell's Ketchup	14 oz.	$.93		☐
	28 oz.	$1.47		☐
	46 oz.	$1.99		☐
3. Willie Stargate Peanut Butter	12 oz.	$1.69		☐
	18 oz. (1 lb. 2 oz.)	$1.93		☐
	28 oz. (1 lb. 12 oz.)	$2.69		☐
4. Princess Cola	2 liter bottle (67.6 fl. oz.)	$1.19		☐
	6 12-fl.-oz. cans	$2.45		☐
5. Wishy-Washy Laundry Detergent	50 oz.	$2.39		☐
Soapy Suds Laundry Detergent	50 oz.	$2.99		☐

Name of Product	Net Weight	Price	Unit Price	Best Buy
6. Uncle Brown's Mustard	24 oz. (1 lb. 8 oz.)	$1.81		☐
Grocery Shop Mustard	20½ oz. (1 lb. 4½ oz.)	$1.49		☐
7. Happy Hawaiian Pineapple Chunks	8 oz.	2 for $.99		☐
Food Mart Pineapple Chunks	8½ oz.	2 for $.89		☐

Supermarket Shopping

 Learner Objectives

Consumer Competencies

- Being able to recognize some advertising techniques used for supermarket products
- Understanding the differences between "store brand" and "national brand"
- Being able to read and compare the weekly newspaper advertisements for supermarkets and being able to determine the best place to shop
- Being able to compare fresh, frozen, canned, and convenience foods for cost and nutritional value
- Being able to recognize and use a coupon

Grammatical Structures

- Being able to understand and use the comparative and superlative

Vocabulary Items

- Being able to understand and use the following words in context:

Nouns	Verbs	Adjectives	
advertiser	advertise	available	fresh
advertising	lie	balanced	frozen
calories	persuade	canned	in-season
convenience	provide	convenient	nutritious
food	taste	cooked	pre-cooked
coupon		cut up	sliced
expiration date		delicious	tasty
fat		economical	
promotion			
protein			
quality			
value			
variety			

 **Dialogue**

(*In the Consumer Education class*) Mr. Wilson, the teacher, comes to class with two bags of groceries.

Mr. Wilson	Now that we know about supermarkets, let's learn how to choose the best and most economical products for you. Look at this jar of peanut butter. Who's on the label?
Quan	Willie Stargate, the famous baseball player.
Mr. Wilson	Look at the ingredients.
Quan	(Reading the label) Peanuts, dextrose, vegetable oil, salt…
Mr. Wilson	Now, look at this store brand of peanut butter. Read the ingredients.
Nilda	Peanuts, dextrose, vegetable oil, salt…Hey, they have the same ingredients.
Mr. Wilson	Right. Now, compare the prices. The two jars are the same size.
Quan	$1.69 for the Willie Stargate brand.
Nilda	The store brand is cheaper. It's only $1.29.
Mr. Wilson	Right, but more people buy the Willie Stargate brand than the store brand.
Nilda	Why?
Mayling	Because people want to eat the same peanut butter that Willie Stargate eats. They think that it's better for you and tastes better.
Mr. Wilson	Right. Advertisers pay Mr. Stargate for permission to put his picture on the label. They pass on the cost of the advertising and promotion to the consumer.
Mayling	That's why store brands are usually cheaper. There's not as much advertising and promotion.
Mr. Wilson	Yes, but don't forget to compare labels and the unit prices. Now, compare these two boxes of cereal, Sugar Crunch and Wheat Flakes.
Althea	(*Comparing the labels*) Sugar Crunch has more sugar than anything else. Wheat Flakes has more wheat. Wheat Flakes is more nutritious and has fewer calories.
Charlie	But, Mr. Wilson, the TV ad says that if you eat Sugar Crunch, you're eating a balanced breakfast.
Mr. Wilson	Think carefully about the ad on TV. What does it show?
Charlie	It shows a bowl of Sugar Crunch with milk and fruit…
Althea	…a glass of juice, a glass of milk, and buttered toast.
Mr. Wilson	Then, it says this breakfast—a bowl of Sugar Crunch with milk and fruit, a glass of juice, a glass of milk, and buttered toast—is a balanced breakfast.
Nilda	Is the ad lying?

Mr. Wilson No, advertisements can't lie. That's the law. But they want to convince you the products they are selling are the best.

Mayling Yes, for example, soft-drink ads always show pictures of young people having fun. You think if you drink that brand, you're going to feel younger and have more fun.

Mr. Wilson Now, look at these two boxes of laundry detergent. One says Super Jumbo size, and the other box says Giant Economy size. Which box is bigger?

Charlie The Super Jumbo size?

Mr. Wilson Let's look at the net weights.

Charlie They're both the same size!

Mr. Wilson Right. Advertisements generally give you very little information about a product. They tell you a product is the tastiest, the most delicious, the biggest, the cheapest, or the most nutritious. But they usually don't give you any facts. They want you to believe you must have a particular product. For example, if you want to feel younger, sexier, or nicer, you should use the product they are selling. Or if Willie Stargate eats the product, it must be good. When you shop, be careful. Be sure that you like the product. And be sure that it's the most economical for you.

■ Comprehension Questions

1. What's the class going to learn about?

   _____

2. Compare the Willie Stargate brand of peanut butter and the store brand. How are they similar? How are they different?

   _____

3. Why do more people buy the Willie Stargate brand?

   _____

4. Why is the Willie Stargate brand more expensive?

   _____

5. Is the store brand always cheaper and of the same quality as the national brand?

   _____

6. Compare Sugar Crunch and Wheat Flakes. How are they different?

   _____

7. Does Sugar Crunch alone provide a balanced breakfast?

_____

8. Compare the Super Jumbo size and the Giant Economy size of laundry detergent. Are they different?

_____

9. What kind of information do advertisements give you?

_____

10. What do they want you to believe?

_____

11. What should you be sure of when you shop?

_____

12. What other methods do advertisements use to persuade you to buy the products they are selling?

_____

Grammar

Comparisons of Inequality

We can show that two people, things, or groups are different in some characteristic by using the comparative form of an adjective or verb. To form the comparative we add *er* to one-syllable adjectives and adverbs and to two-syllable adjectives ending in *y*. Then we form a sentence using *than*.

Adjectives	(tall)	Mr. Franco is tall*er than* Mrs. Franco.
	(short)	Mrs. Franco is short*er than* Mr. Franco.
	(heavy)	Mr. Franco is heavi*er than* Mrs. Franco.*
Adverbs	(fast)	Shirley types fast*er than* Mayling.
	(slow)	Mayling types slow*er than* Shirley.

*In forming the comparative with two-syllable adjectives ending in *y*, the *y* must be changed to *i* before adding *er*.

■ Exercises

A. Make sentences using the comparative form.

Example: Althea is 29 years old. Nilda is 21 years old.

old: <u>Althea is older than Nilda.</u>

young: <u>Nilda is younger than Althea.</u>

1. Mr. Wilson and Quan jog. Mr. Wilson runs fast. Quan runs very fast.

   fast: _____

   slow: _____

2. Saturday the temperature was 60°. Sunday the temperature was 55°.

   warm: _____

   cool: _____

3. Quan and Mayling are having a fight. Quan is angry. Mayling is very angry.

   angry: _____

4. The store brand of peanut butter costs $1.29. The national brand costs $1.69.

   cheap: _____

5. Quan's 5'9". Charlie's 6'.

   tall: _____

   short: _____

6. Charlie's happy today because he doesn't have to work. Nilda's very happy because she can spend the day with Charlie.

   happy: _____

7. Charlie was very busy at work yesterday. He had to fix a lot of cars. Yesterday was a slow day for Nilda at work.

   busy: _____

8. The King Size box of laundry detergent is 5 lb. 4 oz. The Giant Size box is 3 lb. 1 oz.

   large: _____

   small: _____

9. Mr. Franco weighs 200 lb. Mrs. Franco weighs 150 lb.

heavy: _____

light: _____

10. Althea arrived at class at 8 P.M. Quan and Mayling arrived at 8:15 P.M.

early: _____

late: _____

11. Mr. Franco worked hard last week. Mr. Wilson worked very hard.

hard: _____

12. Food Mart's prices are low. Grocery Shop's prices are very low.

low: _____

high: _____

Some adjectives and adverbs have irregular comparative forms.

	Comparative
good	better than
well	better than
bad	worse than
badly	worse than

B. Fill in the blank with the comparative form.

1. People think the Willie Stargate brand of peanut butter is

(good) _____ the store brand.

2. Mr. Franco was sick yesterday. He feels (well) _____ today

_____ he did yesterday.

3. Mr. Franco felt (bad) _____ yesterday _____ he did today.

To make comparisons with other adjectives, adverbs, and nouns, we can say the following:

Adjectives   Wheat Flakes is *more* nutritious *than* Sugar Crunch.
Sugar Crunch is *less* nutritious *than* Wheat Flakes.

Adverbs   Mr. Wilson drives *more* carefully *than* Mr. Franco.
Mr. Franco drives *less* carefully *than* Mr. Wilson.

Nouns   Sugar Crunch has *more* calories *than* Wheat Flakes.
Sugar Crunch has *more* sugar *than* Wheat Flakes.

Count   Wheat Flakes has *fewer* calories *than* Sugar Crunch.

Noncount   Wheat Flakes has *less* sugar *than* Sugar Crunch.

C. Make sentences using the comparative form. Follow the examples.

Example: Wheat Flakes contains a lot of wheat. Sugar Crunch contains some wheat.

wheat:

Wheat Flakes contains more wheat than Sugar Crunch.

Sugar Crunch contains less wheat than Wheat Flakes.

1. The store brand of orange drink contains 15% orange juice. The national brand contains 10% orange juice.

orange juice:

_____

_____

2. The store brand of peanut butter costs $1.29. The Willie Stargate brand costs $1.69.

economical:

_____

_____

3. Quan drinks a cup of coffee for breakfast. Charlie has a bowl of cereal, a glass of juice, and toast.

balanced:

_____

_____

4. Althea went to a party on Saturday. Mr. Wilson worked.

fun:

_____

_____

5. The Willie Stargate brand of peanut butter costs $1.69. The store brand costs $1.29.

expensive:

_____

_____

6. The supermarket sells a lot of jars of the Willie Stargate brand of peanut butter. It sells some jars of its own.

jars:

_____

_____

D. To determine the best place to shop, you should compare several things. Compare these two supermarkets. Which supermarket is better for you?

Food Mart
moderate prices
good variety of products and brands
all products usually available
five miles from your house
can easily get there by bus
can pay by check

Grocery Shop
low prices
fair variety of products and brands
some products not always available
two miles from your house
can't easily get there by bus
can't pay by check

 # Grammar

Comparisons of Equality

When we want to show that two people or things are equal, we can say the following:

Nouns   The Willie Stargate brand of peanut butter is 18 oz. The store brand is also 18 oz.
The Willie Stargate brand is *the same* size as the store brand.
The two jars are *the same* size.

Count	Quan drinks three cups of coffee a day. Mayling drinks three cups of coffee a day.
	Quan drinks *as many* cups of coffee as Mayling.
Noncount	Quan drinks *as much* coffee as Mayling.
Adjectives	José is 23 years old. Charlie is 23 years old.
	José is *as old as* Charlie.
Adverbs	Mr. Wilson drives carefully. Charlie drives carefully.
	Mr. Wilson drives *as carefully as* Charlie.

■ Exercises

Compare Althea and her friend Jane. Use the information below.

Example: Althea and Jane are the same age.
Althea is the same age as Jane.
Althea is as old as Jane.

Althea	**Jane**
29 years old	29 years old
5'5"	5'5"
120 pounds	120 pounds
lives in a one-bedroom apartment	lives in a one-bedroom apartment
gets up at 6:30 A.M.	gets up at 6:30 A.M.
drinks two cups of coffee a day	drinks two cups of coffee a day

 # Grammar

Superlative

To form the superlative we add *est* to adjectives and adverbs that add *er* in the comparative. *The* is placed before the adjective.

Adjectives	Charlie	Mr. Wilson	Quan
	6'	5'11"	5'9"

Mr. Wilson is tall*er* than Quan. (Comparative)
Charlie is the tall*est* of the three. (Superlative)

Adverbs   Mr. Franco goes 65 mph on the highway. Quan goes 60 mph on the highway. Mayling goes 55 mph on the highway.

Quan drives fast*er* than Mayling.
Mr. Franco drives the fast*est*.

To form the superlative with other adjectives and adverbs and nouns we can say the following:

Adjectives
Wheat Flakes is *the most* nutritious cereal in the supermarket.
Sugar Crunch is *the least* nutritious cereal in the supermarket.

Adverbs
Quan drives *the most* carefully.
Mr. Franco drives *the least* carefully.

Nouns
Sugar Crunch has *the most* calories.
Sugar Crunch has *the most* sugar.

Count
Wheat Flakes has *the fewest* calories.

Noncount
Wheat Flakes has *the least* sugar.

Irregular Forms

	Comparative	Superlative
good	better than	the best
well	better than	the best
bad	worse than	the worst
badly	worse than	the worst

■ Exercises

A. The items below are on special this week at these three supermarkets. Compare the unit prices. Which supermarket has the lowest prices this week?

Example:

	Super Market	Food Mart	Grocery Shop
Apples	$1.19/lb.	$5.55/5-lb. bag	$1.21/lb.

The apples at Super Market are cheaper than the apples at Grocery Shop. The apples at Food Mart are the cheapest.

	Super Market	Food Mart	Grocery Shop
Fresh whole chickens	81¢/lb	80¢/lb.	79¢/lb.
Ground beef	$1.79/lb.	$1.59/lb. (3 lb. or more)	$1.25/lb. (5 lb. or more)
Yellow onions	39¢/lb.	$2.00/5-lb. bag	$1.50/4-lb. bag
Lettuce	$1.00/head	99¢/head	$2.90/3 heads
Chunk tuna	$1.01/6½-oz. can	$1.01/6½-oz. can	99¢/6½-oz. can

B. Compare the following kinds of milk in terms of the four categories below.

Whole Milk	Lowfat Milk (2%)	Skim Milk
8 grams fat/8 oz.	5 grams fat/8 oz.	1 gram fat/8 oz.
150 calories/8 oz.	120 calories/8 oz.	100 calories/8 oz.
$1.57/quart	$1.56/quart	$1.47/quart

1. fat _____

_____

2. calories _____

_____

3. price _____

_____

4. taste _____

_____

C. Read the following paragraph.

Fresh, Frozen, or Canned?

How are fresh produce, frozen produce, and canned produce different? Generally, frozen fruits and vegetables are more nutritious than canned. Fresh fruits and vegetables are the most nutritious. Fresh produce can be the cheapest when it's in season. However, when it's not in season, it's usually the most expensive. Some products always cost less when they're frozen, even when they're in season. For example, frozen orange juice is always cheaper than fresh orange juice. Frozen produce and canned produce are more convenient than fresh produce because they keep for a longer time in the freezer or kitchen cabinet. Sometimes, they are easier to prepare because they're already cut up and cooked. However, some people think fresh produce tastes best. Other people like canned or frozen fruits and vegetables better. And others think fresh, frozen, and canned products taste the same.

Based on the reading above, compare fresh, frozen, and canned fruits and vegetables using the following words.

1. nutritious _____

_____

2. cheap _____

_____

3. expensive _____

_____

4. economical _____

_____

5. convenient _____

_____

6. easy _____

_____

7. delicious _____

_____

D. Compare the following items for unit price, taste, and nutrition. (Don't forget that the net weight of canned fruits and vegetables incudes the liquid in the can.)

Example: Fresh spinach is more expensive than canned spinach and frozen spinach, but fresh spinach is the most nutritious.

	Fresh	Frozen	Canned
Mushrooms	$2.49/16 oz.	$1.29/6 oz. (in butter sauce)	$1.05/8 oz. (stems and pieces)
Carrots	59¢/lb.	50¢/10 oz.	49¢/9 oz.
Green Beans	79¢/lb.	49¢/9 oz. (cut)	59¢/16 oz. (cut)
Spinach	89¢/lb.	35¢/10 oz.	59¢/16 oz.
Pears	89¢/lb.		69¢/16 oz. (sliced)

 **Reading**

Coupons

We use coupons to save money on certain products. You can find coupons in the Food section of the newspaper usually on Wednesday or Thursday and Sunday. You should use coupons only for products that you normally buy. You can also use a coupon to try something new. Then, you should buy the smallest size.

Value   Expiration date   Amount   Brand name

Value
The value of the coupon is the money you save when you buy the product and use the coupon. The value is written: "Save 20¢," "15¢ off," or "this coupon worth 25¢." The value of this coupon is 30¢.

Brand Name
The coupon tells you the brand name of the product. This coupon is for Wonderful Brand Sliced Pineapple.

Size or Amount
The coupon tells you the size or amount you must buy to use it. With this coupon you must buy 2 cans of Wonderful Brand Sliced Pineapple.

Expiration Date

The expiration date is the last day you can use the coupon. The expiration date of this coupon is July 20, 1997.

Coupons are usually for national brands. Even with a coupon, the national brand can be more expensive than the store brand. For example, the national brand costs $1.09 for 2 cans, and you have a coupon for 30¢. You pay only 79¢ for the 2 cans. However, the store brand costs $.75 for 2 cans and is of the same quality as the national brand. Therefore, even with a coupon, you pay a higher price for the national brand. Remember to compare unit prices.

■ Comprehension Questions

Write answers to the following questions.

1. Where and when can you find coupons?

   _____

2. When should you use coupons?

   _____

3. What information is on a coupon?

   _____

4. Is the product that you buy with a coupon always the most economical? Why?

   _____

 Reading

Convenience Foods

Convenience foods are sliced, cut up, or pre-cooked foods. Some convenience foods have the ingredients that you need in order to prepare the food in one box or package, for example, a cake mix or frozen broccoli in cheese sauce. Convenience foods take less time to prepare because the manufacturer did most of the preparation for you. However, convenience foods are usually less nutritious and cost more than preparing the food yourself.

If it is important for you to save time, you can use convenience foods. However, if you're interested in better quality, lower costs, and better nutrition, it's better to prepare the food yourself.

■ Comprehension Questions

Write answers to the following questions.

1. What are convenience foods?

   _____

2. Why do convenience foods take less time to prepare?

   _____

3. What are the advantages of convenience foods?

   _____

4. What are the disadvantages of convenience foods?

   _____

 # Listening Comprehension

Listen to your teacher read the following advertisements. Fill in the blanks based on the information in the advertisement.

Example: *Your teachers says:*
At Food Mart this week, large eggs, $1.05/dozen.

You write:

Supermarket: <u>Food Mart</u>_____

Item: <u>large eggs</u>_____   Price: <u>$1.05</u>_____ / <u>dozen</u>_____

1. Supermarket: _____

   Item: _____   Price: _____/_____

2. Supermarket: _____

   Item: _____   Price: _____/_____

3. Supermarket: _____

   Item: _____   Price: _____/_____

4. Supermarket: _____

    Item: _____   Price: _____/_____

5. Supermarket: _____

    Item: _____   Price: _____/_____

6. Supermarket: _____

    Item: _____   Price: _____/_____

7. Supermarket: _____

    Item: _____   Price: _____/_____

8. Supermarket: _____

    Item: _____   Price: _____/_____

9. Supermarket: _____

    Item: _____   Price: _____/_____

10. Supermarket: _____

    Item: _____   Price: _____/_____

Looking for an Apartment

Learner Objectives

Consumer Competencies

- Learning the steps in finding an apartment to rent
- Learning how to read the classified housing ads in the newspaper
- Learning what to consider when deciding on an apartment to rent

Grammatical Structures

- Being able to understand and use the following structures: *would like, will, if…will,* and *may*

Vocabulary Items

Being able to understand and use the following words in context:

Nouns		Verbs	Adjectives
air conditioning	lease	afford	available
appliance	lock	break	furnished/
appointment	manager	inspect	unfurnished
bakery	neighborhood	maintain	reasonable
block	plaster	rent	wall-to-wall
bugs	real estate agency	repair	
carpeting	repairs		
classified ad	security deposit		
cracks	storage area		
damages	suburbs		
efficiency	tenant		
electrical outlet	want ad		
fee	water pressure		
fire escape	water stain		
landlord			

 **Dialogue**

Charlie and Nilda are going to get married soon. They began to look for apartments last week.

(*In the Consumer Education class*)

Nilda Mr. Wilson, Charlie and I looked at apartments all last week.

Charlie We looked everywhere—in the city, in the suburbs...We can't decide. If we rent in the suburbs, we won't be able to take the bus. We'll have to drive. And you know the price of gas!

Nilda And we looked at every kind of apartment—one bedroom, two bedrooms. I can't remember what we've seen. And I'm confused. I don't understand security deposits, leases, and utilities. There must be a better way to look for an apartment!

Mr. Wilson (*Laughing*) Wait a minute! Before you begin looking, you should decide what kind of apartment you'd like and where you'd like to live. If you know what you want, it'll be easier to find a place, and you'll save time.

Nilda I'd like a two-bedroom apartment in the suburbs with a washer and dryer, air conditioning, a club house with a swimming pool, and tennis courts.

Charlie Sure! And I'd like a villa on the French Riviera! Nilda, you know we can't afford that!

Mr. Wilson Did you make a budget? Do you know how much you can afford?

Charlie Well, no.

Mr. Wilson First, decide how much you can afford. An apartment and the utilities should cost about one third of your monthly take-home pay. Then, you should decide what kind of apartment you want—one or two bedrooms, furnished or unfurnished. After you decide what kind of apartment you want, you can begin looking.

Charlie That's a problem. How can we find out about apartments for rent?

Mr. Wilson First, you should decide where you want to live—in the city or the suburbs, which neighborhood, near work, near the bus. Next, get a weekend newspaper and look at the classified ads.

Nilda You mean the want ads?

Mr. Wilson Right.

Althea There are other ways to find out about apartments. Drive or walk around the neighborhoods you like. Look for "for rent" signs. Stop in the neighborhood supermarkets and Laundromats. Sometimes, they have bulletin boards with notices about apartments for rent.

Quan Talk to your friends or people at work. They may know about apartments for rent.

Mayling Some universities have housing offices. They have lists of apartments for rent.

Quan If you're in a hurry, check real estate agencies or apartment rental services. But some of them charge a fee, so you'll probably want to try the other ways first.

Mr. Wilson Let's make a list of the ways to find an apartment: look at the want ads; drive or walk around the neighborhood; talk to friends and people at work; check the housing offices of universities; check real estate agencies or apartment rental services.

■ Comprehension Questions

1. According to Mr. Wilson, what should you do before you begin looking at apartments? Why?

_____

2. What kind of apartment would Nilda like? Is her wish reasonable?

_____

3. How much should an apartment cost?

_____

4. How can Nilda and Charlie find out about apartments for rent?

_____

5. What other ways can Charlie and Nilda find out about apartments for rent?

_____

 # Grammar

Would Like

Would like is a polite way to say *want*. The contractions for *would like* are: I'd, you'd, he'd, she'd, it'd, we'd, you'd, they'd.

We ask:
    Would you like some coffee?
    Would you like to go to the movies?

We usually answer:
    Yes, please.   No, thank you.
    Sure.

The following short answers are not as common:
    Yes, I would.   No, I wouldn't
    Yes, I'd like some.   No, I wouldn't like any.
    Yes, I'd like to.   No, I wouldn't like to.

■ Exercises

A. Fill in the blanks for the questions with *Would you like*. Fill in the answers with *I'd like*.

1. (*In a real estate agency*)
   Manager Can I help you?

   Customer Yes, _____ to rent an apartment.

   Agent _____ to rent a furnished or an unfurnished apartment?
   Customer A furnished apartment.

   Agent How many bedrooms _____?

   Customer One. But _____ something in a safe neighborhood.
   Agent Please fill out this card and sign here.

2. (*In a restaurant*)
   Waiter Are you ready to order?

   Customer No, _____ a few more minutes.
   (*Later*)
   Waiter _____ to order now?

   Customer Yes, _____ the prime rib.

   Waiter How _____ it cooked?
   Customer Medium rare.
   Waiter Soup or salad?
   Customer Salad.
   Waiter What kind of salad dressing _____?
   Customer What kind do you have?
   Waiter French, Thousand Island, Roquefort...
   Customer Roquefort.
   Waiter Coffee?

   Customer No, _____ a cup of tea.

3. (*On the telephone*)
   Landlord Hello.

   Customer Hello. _____ some information on the apartment for rent on Fifth Avenue.
   Landlord It's a one-bedroom, unfurnished apartment for $500 a month.

   Customer _____ to see it.
   Landlord OK. Can you meet me there at one o'clock this afternoon?
   Customer Yes, thank you.

B. Form questions with the following phrases and *Would you like (to)*. Answer the questions.

Example: see a menu

<u>Would you like to see a menu?</u>

<u>Yes, please. or No, thank you. or Yes, I would. or No, I wouldn't.</u>

1. sit down

_____

_____

2. look at a furnished or unfurnished apartment

_____

_____

3. another cup of coffee

_____

_____

4. a one-bedroom or two-bedroom apartment

_____

_____

5. go to a museum or to the zoo tomorrow

_____

_____

C. Answer the question with *I'd like (to)* and the phrase.

Example: (*At a bakery*) May I help you?
Yes, (two dozen oatmeal cookies)

<u>Yes, I'd like two dozen oatmeal cookies.</u>

1. (*At a furniture store*) May I help you?
Yes, (look at a sofa).

_____

2. (*At the library*) May I help you?
Yes, (check out these books).

_____

3. (*At an appliance store*) May I help you?
Yes, (look at a washing machine).

_____

4. (*At the ticket office*) May I help you?
Yes, (two tickets for the symphony on Friday night).

_____

5. (*At an ice cream shop*) May I help you?
Yes, (a double dip of chocolate chip).

_____

D. Role-play the following situations.

1. You want to open a savings account. Tell the bank manager what you want.

2. You want to look at a used car. Tell the salesperson.

3. You want to withdraw $50 from your bank account. Tell the teller.

4. You want to speak to the director for the company. Tell the secretary.

5. You want some information about an apartment for rent. Tell the apartment manager.

6. You're at a fast-food restaurant. You want a double hamburger, small fries, and a large Coke. Tell the waitress or waiter.

E. Newspapers use abbreviations in the want ads in order to save space. You need to understand the abbreviations in order to understand the ad. Look at the following abbreviations.

Apt	apartment		carp	carpeting
a/c	air conditioning		DR	dining room
avail imm	available immediately		effcy	efficiency
BR	bedroom		elec	electricity
blk	block		eves	evenings
bldg	building		exc	excellent

fl	floor	nr	near
furn/unfurn	furnished/unfurnished	prkg	parking
gar	garage	priv	private
ht	heat	refs	references
incl or inc	includes	refrig	refrigerator
kit	kitchen	rm	room
laund	laundry	sec bldg	security building
lge	large	utils	utilities
LR	living room	w/w or ww	wall-to-wall carpeting
loc	location	w/	with

Now, use the abbreviations above to tell what kind of apartment these people would like.

Example: **Steve:** 1BR unfurn suburbs $500/month

Steve would like a one-bedroom, unfurnished apartment in the suburbs for $500 a month.

1. **Robert:** effcy furn nr university $300/month incl utilities

2. **The Hamiltons:** 2BR DR w/w a/c sec bldg w/gar $675/month

3. **SueAnn:** 1 BR unfurn laund nr bus avail imm $490/month

4. **Jorgé:** 2 BR unfurn DR nr school $625/month

F. Read these ads.

   a. Suburban: Lge 1 BR, w/w, laund $525 + elec. 217-3241 eves.

   b. South Hills: 2BR, DR, w/w, nr park and bus $650 + utils. 415-6829

   c. East End: Lg furn 1 rm effcy in priv home. Refs. Nr bus $280. 924-5631

   d. City: 1 BR, 1½ baths w/river view $900 inc ht. Avail imm. 323-4129

Now, match the descriptions below with the right ad.

Example: Tom works in the city but would like to live in the suburbs. He'd like a one-

   bedroom apartment for about $525. <u>Ad a.</u>

1. Ms. Forbes is very rich. She'd like an apartment with a good view. _____

2. Grisel works in the South Hills. She'd like to share an apartment with a friend. Her take-

   home pay is $750 a month. _____

3. Pierre is a student. He doesn't have a lot of money. He'd like to pay about $300 a month

for a furnished apartment. _____

4. Mr. Donovan doesn't have a car. He'd like to live with a family. _____

G. Look at the following ads. Form sentences with _____ *'d like* to match the ads.

Example: South Side: Modern apt. 1 blk bus 1st fl $395

I'd like an apartment for under $400 near the bus. _____

1. West End: Effcy, 1 & 2 BR's avail for May or June, w/w, a/c, sec bldg. Exc loc. 424- 9175

_____

2. Suburban: 1 BR, laund, w/w carp, utils incl $510 prkg. Avail. No children/pets 395-5687

_____

3. North Side: 2nd fl, 1 BR, LR, bath, lge kit, lge refrig. Nr bus May St. $500 + ht 217-9354

_____

4. City: 2 BR a/c, w/w, laund, gar avail $605 incl ht 419-2742

_____

 # Grammar

Will

Will indicates an action in the future. The affirmative contractions are: I'll, you'll, he'll, she'll, it'll, we'll, you'll, they'll. The negative contraction is *won't*.

Question   Will Charlie and Nilda rent an apartment soon?

Answers   Yes, they'll rent an apartment soon.
                  No, they won't rent an apartment soon.

Short Answers   Yes, they will.
                  No, they won't.

Some time-expressions that we use with *will* are:

next week, next month, next year, next Sunday
in a few minutes, in a week, later
tomorrow, the day after tomorrow

■ Exercises

A. In ads, companies make promises about what their products will do for you. Fill in the blanks with *You'll.*

1. Eat Willie Stargate Peanut Butter! _____ feel like a star!

2. Take Ache-less Aspirin! _____ feel better fast!

3. Buy Super Jumbo Clean-O Laundry Detergent! _____ have a cleaner wash,

   and _____ save money!

4. Munch on Munchy Potato Chips! _____ love the taste!

5. Buy Purrrr-fume! _____ feel sexier!

Tell what these products will do for you.

6. Use Silky Hands Dishwashing Liquid!

7. Drive a Speed-O Sports Car!

8. Brush your teeth with Horizon Toothpaste!

B. Before you rent an apartment, you should ask the landlord some questions. Fill in the blanks of these questions with *will.*

1. Who _____ make the repairs?

2. Who _____ paint the apartment?

3. Who _____ fix the appliances (stove, refrigerator, oven) if they break?

4. _____ the landlord raise the rent?

5. How much _____ the utilities cost a month?

C. Fill in the blank in each question with *will*. Fill in the blank in each answer with a pronoun and *will*. Use contractions.

Example: When <u>will</u> Charlie and Nilda make a budget?

<u>They'll</u> make a budget before they look for an apartment.

1. How _____ Charlie and Nilda find out about apartments for rent?

_____ look in the newspaper.

2. When _____ we see you again? _____ see you next week.

3. Where _____ Fred open a bank account? _____ open a bank account at First National Bank.

4. How much money _____ Charlie and Nilda deposit in their savings account?

_____ deposit $50.

5. What _____ Quan buy at the supermarket? _____ buy 10 lb. of laundry detergent.

6. When _____ the store open? _____ open at 10 A.M.

D. Form questions with *will* and the following phrases. Answer the questions.

Example: look for an apartment.

<u>Will Charlie and Nilda look for an apartment tomorrow?</u>

<u>No, they won't. They'll look for an apartment this weekend.</u>

1. rent an apartment

_____

_____

2. go to the supermarket

_____

_____

3. open a bank account

_____

_____

4. cash a check

_____

_____

5. pay your bills

_____

_____

E. Tell what will happen in the future.

Example: Quan's not going to buy steak at the supermarket this week.

<u>He'll buy hamburger.</u>

1. Charlie and Nilda aren't going to look for an apartment today.

_____

2. Quan and Mayling aren't going to clean the house today.

_____

3. Charlie isn't going to finish fixing the car today.

_____

4. Charlie and Nilda aren't going to buy a house.

_____

5. Mr. Franco isn't going to start his diet today.

_____

6. I'm not going to study English this morning.

_____

7. We're not going to the movies tonight.

_____

Grammar

If...Will

We use the expression *if...will* to show that one action depends on another action. The verb after *if* is usually in the present tense. We use *will* in the main part of the sentence.

> If it rains tomorrow, will you go swimming?
> If it rains tomorrow, we won't go swimming.
> If it's sunny tomorrow, we'll go swimming.

We can put the *if-*clause at the beginning or at the end of the sentence:

> If I have time tomorrow, I'll look for an apartment.
> I'll look for an apartment if I have time tomorrow.

■ Exercises

A. Fill in the blanks with *will* or *won't*.

If you decide to rent an apartment, you should first determine what kind of apartment you would like. If you know what you want, it _____ be easier to find a place, and you _____ save time. Careful planning _____ help you. However, you probably _____ find the exact apartment that you want. If you rent an apartment, your main cost _____ be your monthly rent. You _____ also have to pay some utilities. The rent and the utilities should cost about one third of your monthly take-home pay. You probably _____ have to pay a security deposit. The security deposit is usually equal to one or two months' rent. The landlord _____ use the security deposit to pay for repairs of the damages that you cause and to clean the apartment after you leave. He _____ also keep it if you move away from the apartment without paying. If you leave the apartment in good condition, the landlord _____ return your security deposit. If you don't clean your apartment, you _____ probably lose the security deposit.

If you look in the newspaper, you _____ find a list of apartments for rent in the classified ads. When you see an apartment that looks interesting, you should call the landlord or manager (the manager takes care of the apartment building). You should make an appointment to see the apartment.

B. Answer the questions based on the information in the reading.

1. Will you always find the exact apartment that you want?

   _____

2. What will your main cost be if you rent an apartment?

   _____

3. What else will you have to pay?

   _____

4. What will the landlord use the security deposit for?

   _____

5. Will the landlord return your security deposit?

   _____

6. What will you find if you look in the classified ads of the newspaper?

   _____

C. Complete these sentences and questions. Use contractions when possible.

Example: If Charlie and Nilda _rent_____ (rent) an apartment in the suburbs, they'll

   _have_____ (have) to drive to work.

1. If I _____ (have) time, I _____ (call) you tonight.

2. Mayling _____ (wash) the dishes if Quan _____ (do) the laundry.

3. If you _____ (go) to the store, _____ you _____ (buy) some milk?

4. If I _____ (rent) this apartment, how much _____ the rent

   _____ (be)?

5. If it _____ (be) sunny tomorrow, Althea _____ (go) to the beach.

D. Answer the questions.

1. If you go home from class by bus, how long will it take?

_____

2. What will you do if you miss the bus?

_____

3. If you aren't tired, what will you do after class?

_____

4. If you go to the supermarket today, what will you buy?

_____

5. How much will the security deposit be if you rent an apartment?

_____

6. If you don't pay your rent, what will your landlord do?

_____

E. Form question with these phases. Answer them

Example: If it rains this weekend,

   If it rains this weekend, will you go to the movies?

   No, I won't. I'll go to a museum.

1. If Charlie and Nilda open a savings account,

_____

_____

2. If you like the apartment on Fifth Avenue,

_____

_____

3. If Charlie and Nilda rent an apartment near their jobs,

_____

_____

4. If Althea buys a new car,

_____

_____

5. If Charlie and Nilda rent an unfurnished apartment,

_____

_____

 # Grammar

May

May has three meanings.

1. We use *may* to make a request. It is very polite.
Salesperson May I help you?
   Customer Yes, I'd like to look at a color TV.

2. We use *may* to ask permission. It is very polite.
Student May I leave the class early?
Teacher Yes, you may. *or* No, you may not.

3. We use *may* to show possibility.
I'm not sure if I'll go to the beach tomorrow. It may rain.

We use *may* + the simple form of the verb. We use *may* for the present (You *may* go now) and we use *may* for the future (It *may* snow tomorrow).

■ Exercises

A. Fill in the blanks with *may*.

1. It _____ rain tomorrow, but I don't really think it will.

2. Ahmed's mother said he _____ have another cookie.

3. Althea's absent from class this evening. She _____ be sick.

4. Charlie and Nilda can't decide where to rent an apartment. They _____ rent in the city, or they _____ rent in the suburbs.

5. My mother wrote a letter to me three days ago. I _____ receive it today.

6. I'm not sure where Mr. Wilson is. He _____ be in the library.

B. Tell what Charlie and Nilda may do this weekend.

Example: Go to the movies.

_Charlie and Nilda may go to the movies this weekend._____

1. Look for an apartment

_____

2. Go shopping

_____

3. Rent an apartment

_____

4. Look at furniture

_____

5. Go to the mountains

_____

C. Make questions with *may* for the following situations.

Example: You want to leave class early because you don't feel well. Ask the teacher.

_May I leave class early tonight?_____

1. You work in a clothing store. A customer comes in. What do you say?

_____

2. You're knocking on your friend's door. You want to enter the room. What do you say?

_____

3. You want to borrow your boss's pen. What do you say?

_____

4. You're cold. You want to close the window in the classroom. Ask the teacher.

_____

5. You're calling on the telephone. You want to speak to Ms. Forbes. What do you say?

_____

 # Listening Comprehension

Listen to the following conversations. Answer the questions based on the information in the conversations.

A. A conversation between Charlie and the apartment manager.

1. Is Charlie interested in a one- or two-bedroom apartment?

_____

2. Where's it located?

_____

3. Is it furnished?

_____

4. How much is the rent?

_____

5. Does the rent include all utilities?

_____

6. Does Charlie want to see the apartment?

_____

B. A conversation between Denise and the apartment manager.

1. How many bedrooms does the apartment have?

   _____

2. Does the apartment have carpeting?

   _____

3. Does the apartment manager or landlord permit children?

   _____

4. Where's the apartment located?

   _____

5. How much is the rent?

   _____

6. Does Denise want to see the apartment?

   _____

C. A conversation between Robert and the apartment manager.

1. What kind of apartment is it?

   _____

2. Is it furnished?

   _____

3. Is it near the university?

   _____

4. How much is the rent?

   _____

5. Does Robert want to see it? Why?

   _____

 **Reading**

Looking for an Apartment

Before you look at an apartment, you should find out the answers to the following questions by calling the landlord or manager.

How much is the rent?

Is there a security deposit? How much is it? In most cities, the security deposit cannot legally be more than two months' rent.

Are there any other fees, for example, a parking fee or a cleaning fee? Do you have to pay the last month's rent in advance?

Where's the apartment located? Is it near your job, shopping, and the bus?

Is there a lease (a written agreement between you and the landlord)? How long is it for? Can it be broken?

Does the landlord allow children and/or pets?

When you look at an apartment, you should consider the following factors.

Neighborhood
Is the neighborhood safe, clean, quiet, and well-lighted?
Is the apartment close to stores, your job, school, a Laundromat, and the bus?

Building
Is the building clean?
Are there locks on outside doors?
Are there fire escapes?
Are there parking places or a garage? Are they well-lighted?
Are there storage areas, laundry facilities? Are they clean?
Is there a mailbox for each tenant?

Apartment
Do you like the floor plan?
Are the rooms large enough for your furniture?
Are there locks on all outside doors?
Do the windows have locks? Are the windows broken? Do they let in enough air and light?
Do doors and windows open and close easily?
Do the lighting fixtures work? Is there enough light?
Are there enough electrical outlets?
Is the apartment quiet? Can you hear the neighbor's TV or children? Can you hear traffic?
Are the walls, ceilings, and floors in good condition? Do they have cracks, loose plaster, or water stains? Are there drapes and carpets? Are they clean?
Does the heat work? Is there an air conditioner? Does it work?
Are there enough closets, cabinets, and storage areas?
Is the apartment free of bugs?
Do the kitchen appliances work? Who is responsible for repairing them? Are they clean? Is the refrigerator big enough?

Does everything in the bathroom work? Is there enough water pressure? Is there enough hot water?

After you have inspected the apartment, you should try to talk to some of the other tenants. Ask them if there is enough heat and hot water and if the apartment building is free of bugs. Ask them if the landlord maintains the building well and if he makes repairs quickly.

■ Comprehension Questions

1. What should you find out before you look at an apartment?

2. When are your utility bills the highest?

3. How much can the security deposit legally be?

4. What's a lease?

5. What will your initial costs be when you rent an apartment?

6. What should you check in the neighborhood?

7. What should you check in the building?

8. What should you check in the apartment?

9. Why should you try to talk to some of the other tenants?

Renting an Apartment

 Learner Objectives

Consumer Competencies

- Learning the steps in renting an apartment, for example, signing a lease, moving, landlord and tenant responsibilities
- Learning what to do in case of a housing problem

Grammatical Structures

- Being able to understand and use the present perfect tense

Vocabulary Items

- Being able to understand and use the following words in context:

Nouns	Verbs
change-of-address card	forward
credit rating	initial
deposit	notify
rental insurance	promise
initials	run into
installation fee	sublet
liability insurance	
refund	
theft	

 # Dialogue

Secretary (*On the telephone*) Acme Realty Company.

Althea May I speak to Mr. Sellers, please?

Secretary He's not in right now. May I take a message?

Althea Yes. This is Althea Johnson. I live at 1727 Walnut Street. I've called Mr. Sellers several times already about the heat in my apartment. I can't turn it off. Mr. Sellers promised to send someone to fix it, but no one has come yet.

Secretary I'll give him the message.

Althea Thank you. Bye.

(*Althea runs into Mr. Wilson later in the supermarket. They greet each other.*)

Althea Mr. Wilson, do you have a minute? I have a problem with my landlord.

Mr. Wilson Sure, Althea. What's the problem?

Althea It's about 85° outside, and my landlord hasn't turned off the heat yet. I've called him several times, but he hasn't fixed it yet. I know he has to provide adequate heat, but this is ridiculous! It's hotter in my apartment than it is outside.

Mr. Wilson What did he say when you called him?

Althea I talked to him a few weeks ago, and he promised to send someone to repair it within a week. I've called him again several times, but he's never in.

Mr. Wilson Have you written him a letter?

Althea No, I haven't. Should I?

Mr. Wilson Yes. You should write him a letter after you talk to him on the phone. In the letter, repeat what he promised you on the phone. For example: Dear Mr. _____. What's his name?

Althea Sellers.

Mr. Wilson Dear Mr. Sellers,

When we talked yesterday (*give the date*), you promised to send someone to fix the heat within a week. Please tell me when the repairperson is coming.

Sincerely, Althea Johnson

Be sure to keep a copy of the letter.

Althea I'll have to write him a letter immediately. What should I do if he still won't fix it?

Mr. Wilson Then, you can call a lawyer. Laws vary from city to city, so you need to find out the local law. You can also call the Legal Aid Society, a tenants' organization, or the Urban League. They can help you decide what you should do next.

Althea Thanks a lot, Mr. Wilson. You've been a big help.

Mr. Wilson Sure, Althea, good luck.

■ Comprehension Questions

1. Who's Althea calling?

   _____

2. Is he there?

   _____

3. Why is she calling?

   _____

4. Who does Althea see in the supermarket?

   _____

5. Why does Althea want her landlord to turn off the heat?

   _____

6. What did her landlord promise her?

   _____

7. What should Althea write in the letter?

   _____

8. What should Althea do if the landlord still won't fix the heat?

   _____

 # Grammar

Present Perfect

We use the present perfect to show:

1. An action that began in the past and continues to the present:
   Quan has lived in Pittsburgh for five years.

2. An action that occurred at an indefinite time in the past:
   I have visited New York before.

We form the present perfect with the auxiliary *have* and the past participle. The past participle is the same verb form as the past tense for regular verbs.

Affirmative

I have looked	we have looked
you have looked	you have looked
he, she, it has looked	they have looked

Contractions: I've, you've, he's, she's, it's, we've, you've, they've

Negative

I have not looked	we have not looked
you have not looked	you have not looked
he, she, it has not looked	they have not looked

Contractions: I haven't, you haven't, he hasn't, she hasn't, it hasn't, we haven't, you haven't, they haven't

Question Form

Have I looked?	Have we looked?
Have you looked?	Have you looked?
Has he looked?	Have they looked?
Has she looked?	
Has it looked?	

Short Answers

Affirmative	Negative
Yes, I have.	No, I haven't.
Yes, you have.	No, you haven't.
Yes, he has.	No, he hasn't.
Yes, she has.	No, she hasn't.
Yes, it has.	No, it hasn't.
Yes, we have.	No, we haven't.
Yes, they have.	No, they haven't.

Some irregular verbs have the same forms for the past and the past participles (see *find*). Other irregular verbs have a past participle form that is different from its present and past (see *write*). Those that are used in this unit are as follows:

Present	Past	Past Participle
be	was, were	been
buy	bought	bought
come	came	come
do	did	done
find	found	found
make	made	made
read	read	read
see	saw	seen
teach	taught	taught
write	wrote	written

■ Exercises

A. Fill in the blanks with the correct form of the verb in the present perfect.

Example: Charlie and Nilda <u>have looked</u>_____ (look) at apartments all week.

1. Quan and Mayling _____ (live) in Pittsburgh for five years.

2. The class _____ already _____ (learn) about shopping in supermarkets.

3. Althea _____ (attend) the consumer education class since October.

4. Charlie and Nilda _____ recently _____ (look) in the want ads for apartments for rent.

B. Fill in the blanks with the negative form of the verb in the present perfect.

Example: I <u>haven't listened</u>_____ (listen) to the radio for three days.

1. Mr. and Mrs. Franco _____ (watch) TV all evening.

2. Charlie and Nilda _____ (call) about the apartment on Grant Street yet.

3. Mayling _____ (teach) for several years.

C. Form questions in the present perfect tense. Answer them.

Example: How long <u>have you lived</u>_____ (live) in your house?

1. How long _____ (study) English?

2. How long _____ (work) at your present job?

3. How many apartments _____ (look) at this week?

4. How long _____ (live) in the United States?

5. How many times _____ (be) to a baseball game?

6. How many questions _____ (answer) so far?

D. Answer the questions with a short answer.

Example: Have you lived in Pittsburgh all your life?

Yes, I have.

1. Have you lived in the United States for a long time?

_____

2. Have you studied English for a long time?

_____

3. Has your English improved since you've been in the United States?

_____

4. Have you ever visited Canada?

_____

5. Have Charlie and Nilda looked for an apartment lately?

_____

6. Have you done your laundry recently?

_____

7. Have you seen a good movie lately?

_____

E. Form questions with *How long*. Answer them with *for* or *since*.

Example: Jane is Althea's friend. She has been Althea's friend for five years.

How long has Jane been Althea's friend?

She's been Althea's friend for five years.

1. Quan and Mayling live in Pittsburgh. They moved to Pittsburgh five years ago.

_____

_____

2. Mayling's a university professor. In 1989, she began working at the university.

_____

_____

3. Mr. Wilson teaches the Consumer Education class. He began teaching the class in October.

_____

_____

4. Charlie's an auto mechanic. He began working as an auto mechanic three years ago.

_____

_____

5. José studies English. He began studying English three years ago.

_____

_____

F. Ask your classmates questions with _How long_ and these phrases.

Example: live in Pittsburgh

<u>How long have you lived in Pittsburgh?</u>

1. study English

_____

2. be in the U.S.

_____

3. live at your present address

_____

4. be married

_____

G. Althea has decided to look for a new apartment because she doesn't like her landlord, and she wants a larger apartment. Ask questions to find out if she's done the following things to look for an apartment. Answer the questions.

Example: look in the newspaper

Has Althea looked in the newspaper yet?

Yes, she's already looked in the newspaper.

No, she hasn't looked in the newspaper yet.

1. read the want ads

_____

Yes, _____

2. walk around the neighborhood

_____

Yes, _____

3. talk to friends and people at work

_____

Yes, _____

4. call a real estate agency

_____

No, _____

5. check the housing office at the university

_____

No, _____

6. find an apartment

_____

No, _____

7. sign a lease

_____

No, _____

H. Charlie and Nilda have finally found an apartment. Charlie is getting ready to move out of his old apartment and into the new one. Ask questions to find out what he has already done and what he hasn't done yet. Answer the questions.

Example: open a bank account near his new apartment

   Has Charlie opened a bank account near his new apartment yet?

   No, he hasn't.

1. notify magazine publishers of his new address

_____

Yes, _____

2. write to friends to tell them his new address

_____

Yes, _____

3. change the address on his driver's license

_____

No, _____

4. call the telephone company

_____

Yes, _____

> **NOTE:** Charlie doesn't have to pay the telephone company a deposit because he has always paid his telephone bills on time. He has a good credit rating with the telephone company. He will have to pay the telephone company a fee to begin telephone service in his new apartment. This is called an installation fee.
>
>   If you've never had a telephone in your own name, the company will probably ask you to pay a deposit for new service.

5. call the electric company

_____

Yes, _____

6. make notes on the condition of the apartment.

_____

Yes, _____

> **NOTE:** Before you move into an apartment, make notes on the condition of the apartment, the appliances, and any furniture included in the apartment. If possible, ask the landlord to look at the apartment with you. Sign and date the notes. Ask the landlord to sign them also. Keep a copy and give one to the landlord.

7. buy rental insurance for the new apartment.

_____

No, _____

> **NOTE:** It is a good idea to get rental insurance to protect your personal property against fire and theft. Rental insurance can also include liability insurance. Liability insurance protects you if someone has an accident in your apartment. You can buy rental insurance if you rent an apartment or a house.

8. pay the rent and security deposit for the new apartment.

_____

Yes, _____

9. receive the security deposit from the landlord of his old apartment.

_____

No, _____

10. fill out a change-of-address card

_____

Yes, _____

NOTE: The change-of-address card is a form you fill out at the post office. The post office will forward your mail. This means they will send your mail to your new address if it has your old address on it.

I. Here is a copy of the change-of-address card that Charlie filled out. Answer the questions.

U.S. Postal Service **CHANGE OF ADDRESS ORDER**	Instructions: Complete Items 1 thru 10. You must SIGN Item 9. Please PRINT all other items including address on face of card.	**OFFICIAL USE ONLY** Zone/Route ID No.

1. Change of Address for: *(Check one)*
   ☒ Individual ☐ Entire Family ☐ Business
2. Start Date: Month 0 6 Day 2 5 Year 9 6

Date Entered on Form 3982
M M D D Y Y

3. Is This Move Temporary? *(Check one)*
   ☒ No ☐ Yes, Fill in ▶
4. If TEMPORARY move, print date to discontinue forwarding: Month Day Year

Expiration Date
M M D D Y Y

5. Print Last Name *(include Jr., Sr., etc.)* or Name of Business *(If more than one, use separate form for each).*
   W I S N I C K

Clerk/Carrier Endorsement

6. Print First Name *(or Initial)* and Middle Name *(or Initial).* Leave blank if for a business.
   C H A R L E S

7a. For Puerto Rico Only: if OLD mailing address is in Puerto Rico, print urbanization name, if appropriate.

7b. Print OLD mailing address: House/Building Number and Street Name (include St., Ave., Rd., Ct., etc.).
   4 1 2   4 0 T H   S T R E E T

Apt./Suite No.   or   PO Box No.   or ☐RR/☐HCR *(Check one)*   RR/HCR Box No.

City P I T T S B U R G H   State P A   ZIP Code 1 5 2 2 2 - ZIP+4 4 3 7 0

8a. For Puerto Rico Only: if NEW mailing address is in Puerto Rico, print urbanization name, if appropriate.

8b. Print NEW mailing address: House/Building Number and Street Name (include St., Ave., Rd., Ct., etc.).
   5 9 2   G R A N T   S T R E E T

Apt./Suite No. A P T   4   or   PO Box No.   or ☐RR/☐HCR *(Check one)*   RR/HCR Box No.

City P I T T S B U R G H   State P A   ZIP Code 1 5 2 1 9 - ZIP+4 7 6 0 6

9. Signature: *(See conditions on reverse)*
   Charles Wisnick
10. Date Signed: Month 0 6 Day 1 9 Year 9 6

OFFICIAL USE ONLY
Verification Endorsement

PS FORM **3575**, November 1995

1. Who filled out the card?

   _____

2. What's Charlie's old address?

   _____

3. What's his new address?

   _____

4. When does Charlie want the post office to begin forwarding his mail?

_____

5. When did Charlie fill out the card?

_____

6. Is the change-of-address for Charlie and his family or only for him?

_____

J. Ask your classmates if, any time in their lives, they have done the following things.

Example: go to the zoo

Have you ever gone to the zoo?
No, never. or Yes, I have. or No, I haven't.

1. fill out a change-of-address card

2. call the telephone company

3. buy rental insurance

4. sign a lease

5. write a letter of complaint to your landlord

6. be late for class

7. sail a boat

8. see a tornado

 Listening Comprehension

Listen to the following conversations. Answer the questions based on the information in the conversation.

A. Mr. Sellers, Althea's landlord, calls her on the phone.

1. Who's calling Althea?

_____

2. Why is he calling?

_____

3. When will the repairperson be at Althea's apartment?

_____

4. Will Althea be there?

_____

B. Charlie's talking on the phone with the landlord.

1. Why is Charlie calling Mr. Lesser?

_____

2. When should Charlie be at Mr. Lesser's office?

_____

3. Why is Charlie going to Mr. Lesser's office?

_____

C. Charlie calls an insurance company to find out some information about rental insurance for the new apartment.

1. What's the first question the insurance agent asks Charlie?

_____

2. How many apartment units are there in Charlie and Nilda's building?

_____

3. What floor do Charlie and Nilda live on?

_____

4. Is the building brick or frame?

_____

5. How much will personal property insurance cost?

_____

6. How much more will liability insurance cost?

Reading

Leases

A lease is a written agreement between the landlord and tenant. Be sure you read the lease carefully *before* you sign it. Never sign a lease that you can't read. If you need help in reading the lease, you can call one of the following. They'll help you.

1. a lawyer
2. the Urban League
3. the Legal Aid Society or Neighborhood Legal Services
4. tenants' organizations

A lease should contain the following information:

1. Your name and the address of the apartment.
2. The name, address, and telephone number of the landlord and the manager.
3. How much rent you must pay and to whom you must pay it.
4. When the rent is due.
5. How long the lease is for; when it begins and when it ends.
6. How much the security deposit is; if there are any other fees.
7. What utilities you must pay; what utilities the landlord must pay.

The landlord and tenant have responsibilities. The lease will usually list these responsibilities.

Tenant Responsibilities

1. You must pay your rent on time.
2. You must take care of the apartment. Don't put holes in the walls, paint the floor, etc.
3. You must not cause fire or health problems.

Before you sign the lease, you should find out:

- if you can sublet the apartment;
- what will happen if you break the lease;
- if you can have children or pets in the apartment;
- what repairs you will be responsible for;
- if you have any other responsibilities.

Landlord Responsibilities

1. The landlord must take care of the building and grounds. For example, he must cut the grass, repair the roof, etc.
2. The landlord must provide heat, hot water, and keep the building free of bugs. That is the law.
3. The lease will tell you when the landlord can enter your apartment.

Before you sign the lease, find out what repairs the landlord will be responsible for.

If you or the landlord wants to change the lease, write the changes on the lease. You and the landlord should initial the changes (your initials are the first letters of your full name). Also, if the landlord makes any promises, for example, if he promises to paint the apartment before you move in, write it on the lease and initial it. Never sign a lease that has any blank spaces.

After you understand the lease completely, you and the landlord should sign two copies. You keep a copy, and the landlord keeps a copy.

At the end of the lease, the landlord can: (1) raise the rent; (2) ask you to move: (3) renew your lease. Of course, you may decide to move. If you decide to move, you should go through the apartment with the landlord to determine the damages that you are responsible for. In many states, the law requires the landlord give you:

1. a list of any repairs that you are responsible for;
2. a refund of your security deposit less the cost of repairs on the list. This must be done within 30 days of your move.

■ Comprehension Questions

Write the answers to the following questions.

1. What's a lease?

   _____

2. Should you sign a lease that you don't understand?

   _____

3. What should you do if you don't understand a lease?

   _____

4. What information should a lease contain?

   _____

5. What responsibilities does a tenant have?

   _____

6. What should you find out before you sign a lease?

   _____

7. What responsibilities does the landlord have?

   _____

8. What should you do if you or the landlord changes the lease or if the landlord makes any promises?

   _____

9. When should you sign the lease?

   _____

10. What's the law in your city or state concerning security deposits?

    _____

Buying Furniture and Appliances

 Learner Objectives

Consumer Competencies

- Learning the steps involved in buying furniture and appliances
- Learning about the different types of stores where you can buy furniture and appliances
- Being able to recognize different sales tactics

Grammatical Structures

- Review of the following verb tenses: present; present continuous; past; past continuous; future (*going to* + verb; *will* + verb); and present perfect

Vocabulary Items

- Be able to understand and use the following words in context:

Nouns		Verbs	Adjective
annual percentage rate	finance charge	fire	reputable
charge account	finance company	measure	
complaint	fine print		
consumer guides	garage sale		
credit	installation		
credit contract	installment plan		
credit plan	interest rates		
delivery	manufacturer		
department store	model		
discount store	operation		
down payment	second hand store		
durability	service		
fee	speciality store		
	warranty		

 **Dialogue**

(*In the Consumer Education class*)

Charlie   Mr. Wilson, Nilda and I have decided to buy a sofa for our new apartment. Can you tell us how to go about looking for one?

Mr. Wilson   Weren't you going to rent a furnished apartment?

Charlie   We were, but we compared the cost of renting a furnished apartment with the cost of buying furniture. We've saved some money. We're going to get wedding gifts, and our parents are going to give us some things. So we decided to rent an unfurnished apartment. It'll be cheaper in the long run. And if we buy a house someday, we'll already have furniture.

Quan   Mr. Wilson, Mayling and I want to buy a washing machine and dryer. With the baby coming, we'll need them.

Althea   And I want to buy a TV. How do we go about buying these things?

Mr. Wilson   Basically, you follow the same steps to buy a sofa, a washing machine, or a TV. First, you must decide if you really need what you're thinking about buying.

Nilda
Quan   (*Together*) Yes!
Althea

Mr. Wilson   OK. Then, let's discuss how to go about buying furniture and appliances and where to buy them. There are four basic steps: decide how much you can or want to spend; plan before you shop; learn everything you can about the product; compare prices and services at different stores.

Nilda   This will be a big help.

Charlie   Yes. Then, after we find out how to shop and where to shop, all we have to do is figure out how to pay for it!

■ Comprehension Questions

1. Why did Nilda and Charlie decide to rent an unfurnished apartment?

_____

2. What do Quan and Mayling want to buy? Why?

_____

3. What does Althea want to buy?

_____

4. What do you have to decide first before you buy furniture and appliances?

_____

5. What are the basic steps for buying furniture and appliances?

_____

6. What does Charlie want to know after he finds out how and where to shop?

_____

 # Grammar

Tense Review

A. Fill in the blanks with the correct form of the verb.

Althea _is going_____ (go) to a department store today to look for a TV. She

_____ (have) a charge account at the department store, so she _____

(know) if she _____ (find) a TV, she can _____ (use) her credit card.

The department store _____ (have) a good variety of TV's, and it

_____ (offer) many services.

 Yesterday, Althea _____ (go) to a specialty store. A speciality store

_____ (carry) one or a few different items. Some speciality stores

_____ (have) lower prices, and others _____ (have) higher prices.

They usually _____ (offer) good services. Althea can _____ (uses)

her credit card at a specialty store or the store's credit plan. They _____ (have)

the same interest rates.

 Althea can also _____ (look) for a TV at a discount store. A discount store

usually _____ (sell) products at lower prices. Sometimes, a discount store

_____ (not offer) as many services as a department store. And, sometimes, the

products in a discount store _____ (not be) as good as those in a department store. Althea _____ (know) that she must _____ (shop) carefully at a discount store.

Tomorrow, Althea _____ (call) a discount store to compare prices and services. After Althea compares prices and services at all the different stores, she _____ (wait) a few weeks to see if the TV _____ (go) on sale. Sometimes, TV's _____ (be) cheaper on sale at a department store than anywhere else.

Answer the questions based on the story.

1. Where is Althea going today? Why?

_____

2. What is the advantage of buying a TV at the department store?

_____

3. Where did Althea go yesterday?

_____

4. How can Althea pay for a TV at a specialty store?

_____

5. What are the differences between a discount store and a department store?

_____

6. Why should Althea shop carefully at a discount store?

_____

7. What will Althea do after she compares prices and services at the different stores?

_____

8. When are TV's likely to be reasonably priced at a department store?

_____

B. Here is some information about Quan. Answer the questions about Quan's life.

1966	1972–1984	1988	1991
born in New York	student in New York	became an architect	got married, moved to Pittsburgh

1. When did Quan live in New York?

   _____

2. What did he do in New York?

   _____

3. How long has Quan been an architect?

   _____

4. How long has Quan been married?

   _____

5. How long has he lived in Pittsburgh?

   _____

C. Here is some information about Mayling's life. Imagine you are a reporter. Interview Mayling. Ask her questions about her life. Ask her questions about her future.

1967	1971	1981–1985
born in Ohio	family moved to Illinois	went to North High School

1985–1988	1988	1989–1990
attended the University	traveled to Europe for six months	attended a university in New York

1991	1991–present
got married and moved to Pittsburgh	professor at a university in Pittsburgh

D. Rewrite this story in the past tense. Change *Althea* to *Nilda and Charlie*. Change the sentence *Now, she's at the store* to *Yesterday, they went to the store.*

Althea has called many stores and gone to many stores to look for a TV. She has compared the stores' prices, services, and credit plans. She has finally decided which TV she wants to buy and where she wants to buy it. Now, she's at the store. She is discussing the credit plan with the salesperson. The credit contract lists the finance charge and the annual percentage rate (APR) of interest. The finance charge includes the interest and all the other fees for using credit. The interest (APR) in Althea's credit contract is 18%. Althea's reading the contract carefully. She's asking a lot of questions about the "fine print." She wants to make sure she understands the contract. She wants to make sure she knows exactly how much money she has to pay back. Before she signs the contract, she's going to make sure there are no blank spaces.

Althea's going to give the store a cash down payment. When she signs the contract, she's going to promise to pay the rest of the costs of the TV, the interest, and the finance charge in equal monthly payments (the installment plan).

E. Fill in the blanks to complete the dialogues.

Example: **Quan** Where <u>have you been</u> _____ all morning?
                Mayling I went to some garage sales.

        Quan Oh, no! <u>What did you buy?</u> _____
     Mayling I don't know what it is, but isn't it pretty!
        Quan Mayling, you complain about the way I shop at supermarkets. Look how you waste money at garage sales!

1. **Mayling** Where _____ since 10 A.M.?
      Quan I went to a few secondhand stores.

   Mayling _____?
      Quan To look for a washing machine.

   Mayling _____ a new one.
      Quan Used machines are cheaper.
   Mayling But Quan, you don't know anything about washing machines!

      Quan _____

NOTE: Secondhand stores and garage sales are good places to buy used things at low prices. Sometimes, you can save a lot of money. But you should know what to look for. If you buy a used washing machine at a garage sale, it won't have a warranty. If something goes wrong with it, you can't return it.

2. **Quan** Where _____ this morning?
   Mayling I was at the library.

   Quan _____?
   Mayling I was reading *Consumer Reports* about washing machine and dryers. It has a lot of information. You should read it, Quan.

3. **Charlie** _____?
   Nilda I'm calling the Better Business Bureau.

   Charlie _____?
   Nilda I want some information about the store we went to yesterday.

   Charlie _____
   Nilda I want to know if there have been any complaints against the store.

4. **Mayling** _____?
   Quan I'm looking in the Yellow Pages for names of stores that sell appliances. I'm going to call them to compare prices.

   Mayling _____?
   Quan Yes, I have. I checked the newspaper this morning for stores that have washing machines on sale.

NOTE: To save time and gas, use your telephone to compare prices and services. You can find the names and location of furniture and appliance stores in the Yellow Pages of the telephone book. The Yellow Pages lists almost every business in your city. You can also check the newspapers. The newspapers have ads for stores that have appliances and furniture for sale. Often, the ads give the manufacturer's name, the model number, the price of the item, and sometimes the special features.

Before you call a store, you should know the name of the item, the manufacturer, the model number, and the color and size you want.

5. **Charlie** _____ an hour ago? I was looking for you.

   Nilda _____

6. _____ ever _____?

   No, _____

7. How long _____?

   _____ since 4 o'clock!

8. _____ tomorrow?

   No, I can't _____

9. **Mr. Wilson** Would you like to go to the movies tonight?

   Althea _____

   Mr. Wilson How about Saturday night?

   Althea _____

10. **Althea** Mr. Wilson, I had a wonderful time Saturday night.

   Mr. Wilson _____

 # Reading

The Consumer Education class made this list of the steps for buying furniture and appliances.

1. Decide how much you can or want to spend on the furniture or the appliance.

2. Plan before you shop.

  • Find out if you have a gas or electric connection in your house for the appliance.
  • Measure the space available for the appliance or furniture. Don't buy a sofa that fits in your living room but doesn't fit through your front door.

3. Learn everything you can about the product.

  • Ask your family and friends if they can recommend a brand or model.
  • Check *Consumer Reports* and other consumer guides. These are available in the library. *Consumer Reports* compares products and describes their advantages and disadvantages based on tests.
  • Decide what feature you want. For example, do you really need all the extras on the deluxe model washing machine?
  • Compare operation and service costs of different brands and models.
  • Talk to salespeople. Ask questions about the safety and durability (how long it will last) of the product.
  • Read the labels. Look for appliances that meet the National Standard for Safety. Look for these seals: UP on electrical appliances and AGA on gas appliances. They mean that the product is safe. Furniture should have a tag that states the contents.
  • Compare warranties (or guarantees). A warranty tells what the manufacturer or seller will do if something goes wrong with the product within a certain amount of time.
  • Read the instructions in the operating manual.

4. Compare prices and services.

- Ask your family and friends if they can recommend a store.
- Check the prices at several stores. Look for sales. Remember, a higher price doesn't always mean better quality.
- Compare the services at several stores:
     delivery
     installation
     repair service
- Find out if delivery and installation are included in the price.
- Only deal with reputable stores. You can call the Better Business Bureau to check on a store.

■ Comprehension Questions

Write the answers to the following questions.

1. What's the first step for buying furniture or appliances?

    _____

2. Before you buy furniture or an appliance, why should you measure your door at home?

    _____

3. What should you ask your family and friends?

    _____

4. What's *Consumer Reports*? Where can you find it?

    _____

5. Why should you compare operation costs of different brands and models?

    _____

6. What should you ask salespeople?

    _____

7. What seals can you find on appliances? What do they mean?

    _____

8. What's a warranty?

    _____

9. Does higher price always mean that the appliance or furniture is better?

_____

10. What services are available at some stores?

_____

11. What's the Better Business Bureau? Why should you call it?

_____

Listening Comprehension

Listen to the following conversations. Answer the questions based on the information in the conversation.

A. Charlie's in a furniture store. He's looking for a sofa. He's talking to the salesperson.

1. How much is the sofa that the store advertised in the newspaper?

_____

2. What's wrong with it?

_____

3. How much is the other sofa?

_____

4. Should Charlie buy a sofa from this store?

_____

B. Quan's in an appliance store looking for a washing machine. He's talking to the salesperson.

1. How much is the washing machine?

_____

2. How long will it be on sale?

_____

3. Does Quan need all the special features?

_____

4. What will happen to the price of the washing machine tomorrow?

_____

5. Should Quan buy this washing machine?

_____

C. Nilda's in a store looking for a sofa. She's talking to the salesperson.

1. How much is the sofa?

_____

2. How much is the down payment?

_____

3. How much is the weekly payment?

_____

4. How long do you make the weekly payments?

_____

5. Should Nilda buy a sofa from this store?

_____

D. Althea is in a store looking for a TV. She's talking to the salesperson.

1. How much is the TV?

_____

2. Why does the salesperson say that Althea should buy the TV now?

_____

3. Should Althea buy a TV from this store?

_____

E. Althea's at another store looking for a TV. She's talking to the salesperson.

1. How much was the TV that the store advertised in the newspaper?

   _____

2. When did the store advertise the TV?

   _____

3. Can Althea buy it? Why?

   _____

4. How much is the TV that the salesperson is showing her?

   _____

5. Should Althea buy a TV from this store?

   _____

19 ROSWELL